CONTENTS

Introduction

Chapter 1 –Buying a Home-Looking for a Home   **13**

Area   13

Choosing your property   14

Valuing a property   15

Purchasing a flat   15

Problems with Airbnb   18

Viewing properties   19

Buying an old house   20

Renovation grants   20

Disabled facilities grant   21

Equalities Act 2010   21

Planning permission   21

Buying a listed building   22

Buildings in conservation areas   22

Buying a new house or flat   23

Building Guarantees   25

Withholding payments   25

Websites for house builders   26

Buying a Rented House-Right to Buy   26

If your landlord has spent money on your home   27

Social Homebuy   28

Buying more of your home later   28

Help to Buy Schemes   29

Shared/part ownership property   29

Self-build property   30

Chapter 2-The Role of Estate Agents in Buying   33

and Selling Property

Estate Agents   33

What to expect from an estate agent   34

Choosing an agent if selling   35

Sole agency selling   35

Joint sole agents   36

Multiple agency   36

Buying property using the internet   36

Selling property using the internet   42

Ten top tips when selling a property   43

Chapter 3- Buying a Property-The Practicalities   45

How to speed up home sales   45

Considerations when buying a house or flat   48

Budgeting   48

Deposits   48

Stamp duty- What is stamp duty and who pays it?   49

How much do I have to pay?   49

Rates on your first home   49

A STRAIGHTFORWARD GUIDE
TO
BUYING AND SELLING YOUR OWN HOME

FRANCES JAMES

Editor: Roger Sproston

Straightforward Publishing
www.Straightforwardco.co.uk

77000016002 8

British cataloguing in Publication Data. A Catalogue record of this publication is available in the British Library.

ISBN:
978-1-80236-026-4

4edge www.4edge.co.uk

Cover design by BW Studio Derby

Other costs   52

Land Registry   52

Energy Performance Certificates (EPC's)   53

Structural surveys   53

Mortgage fees-Mortgage indemnity insurance.   55

Mortgage arrangement fees   55

Buildings insurance   56

Removals   56

Costs of moving   57

The process of buying a property   58

Making an offer   58

Putting your own home on the market   59

Exchange of contracts   59

Buying with a friend   60

Completing a sale   60

Buying at auction   60

What is a property auction?   61

Different types of property auction houses   61

Those who attend auctions   62

What types of property are suitable for auction?   63

Why is property being sold at an auction?   63

What happens next?   64

Bidding for a property   65

Bidding from your smart phone   66

How do prospective purchasers find out legal 67
and survey information for properties?

How is finance arranged? 68

Can lots be bought before auction? 68

House swapping 69

Saving money through swapping homes 69

Chapter 4- More About Mortgages **71**

Lenders-Banks and building societies 71

Centralised lenders 72

Brokers and "independent" financial advisors 72

How much can you borrow? 73

Mortgage Market Review 73

Deposits 77

Help to Buy equity loan 77

Buying through shared ownership 79

Older people 80

Disabled people 80

Buying more shares 81

Selling your home 81

Joint mortgages 82

Main types of mortgage 82

Endowment 82

Repayment mortgages 83

Pension mortgages 84

Interest only mortgage   84

Mixed mortgages   84

Foreign currency mortgages   84

Cashbacks   85

Buy to Let Mortgages   85

Using price comparison websites   88

Plan for times when there's no rent coming in   88

What to do if you feel that you have been given   89
wrong advice

Borrowing and the internet   91

Chapter 5-Selling Your Home   **93**

Estate agents   93

DIY Selling   93

Setting the price if selling yourself   93

Advertising your property independently   94

Selling using online agents   94

Rights when using an online estate agent   95

Pros and cons of online estate agents   98

Selling at Auction   100

Advantages of auction   100

Chapter 6-Conveyancing a Property   **103**

Legal ownership of property   103

Freehold property   104

Leasehold property   105

The lease-Preamble   105

Check points   108

Two systems of conveyancing   108

Registered and unregistered land   109

Registered land   109

Production of the Land Certificate   111

The key steps in the process of conveyancing property   111

Making enquiry's before contract   111

Local land charges search   113

Local authority searches   115

Coal mining search   116

Other enquiries   117

Planning matters relating to specific properties 117

The contract for sale   118

Procedures in the formation of contract   119

The Contents of a contract   119

Miss-description   120

Misrepresentation   121

Non-disclosure   122

Signing the contract   123

Exchanging contracts   123

Completion   124

Return of pre-contract deposits   125

The position of the parties after exchange of contracts   125

Bankruptcy of the vendor   125

Bankruptcy of the purchaser   126

Death of Vendor or purchaser   126

Chapter 7-Planning Moving Arrangements   **129**

DIY moves   129

Using professionals   130

Contacting utilities   131

Chapter 8-Buying and Selling in Scotland   **133**

Looking for property   133

Newspapers   133

Estate agents   133

Home reports in Scotland   134

Making an offer on a Scottish property   134

Conveyancing for buyers in Scotland   135

Concluding the missives   136

Land and Buildings Transaction Tax   136

Buying a tenement property   137

Tenement maintenance costs   137

What is a 'factor'?   138

Restrictions of use   138

Feuhold properties and feu duty   138

Joint ownership of a Scottish property   139

Joint ownership   139

Common property   139

Help to Buy (Scotland)   139

How the Scottish property system differs from the 140
rest of the UK

Chapter 9-Buying Overseas   **141**

General   141

European property   142

Other useful websites: 142

The USA   142

Property overseas generally   143

Useful information and websites

Glossary of terms

Index

****

INTRODUCTION

As time goes by, we either find ourselves in the middle of a housing market 'boom' or a 'bust'. Currently, at the time of writing, **2022,** we are experiencing an erratic cycle in house prices, the London market is growing in certain areas and contracting in others due, it is said, to a lack of new housing. Whatever the cause, home ownership is beyond the reach of many in the South East generally. Other areas outside of London and the South East are showing signs of growth.

There are several other factors now to be considered when buying and selling a home. The first is the advent of COVID 19 and the effect this has had on the conveyancing of a sale or purchase, i.e. the fact that the time taken to convey the property has now lengthened considerably. This has lessened somewhat as the pandemic and the subsequent lockdowns have eased. The second consideration has been the increased attention on energy performance and the need for homeowners to ensure that their homes are fully insulated to achieve the highest energy rating possible. The eventual replacement of gas boilers, to be replaced by Heat Pumps is on the agenda in 2022. This will be discussed further on.

However, notwithstanding market conditions, the process of buying and selling a home remains probably the single most important activity undertaken by individuals in their lifetime. The money and effort involved means that it is a process that must be carried out effectively and with a clear knowledge of the elements involved.

There are different people out there buying property, some private individuals and other buy-to-let investors. This book is aimed generally at those who are trying to buy and sell a property regardless of their ultimate intentions.

When buying or selling a home, particularly buying, you will liase with a whole number of people, professional or otherwise: solicitors, estate agents, finance brokers, surveyors, banks and building societies and so on. All of these people play a vital role in the house purchase/sale transaction. All of these parties involved will have many years experience of property and not all of them will be acting in your own best interests.

Very often, the person who owns the property or who wishes to purchase a property is the one with the least knowledge of the process and is the one who stands to lose the most. When initially looking for a property, wrong decisions are made. The price paid for a property is quite often too high, with disastrous consequences later on. The condition of the property may leave a lot to be desired. There are many stories of people losing out on this single most important transaction. Unfortunately, it is a fact that if mistakes are made at the outset then you might spend the rest of your life recovering from the consequences.

****

Chapter 1

Buying a Home-Looking for a Home

___

Obviously, where you choose to buy your house will be your own decision. However, it may be your first time and you may be at a loss as to where to buy, i.e. rural areas or urban areas, the type and cost of property or whether a house or flat. There are several considerations here:

Area

Buying in a built up area has its advantages and disadvantages. There are normally more close communities, because of the sheer density. However, it is true to say that some built up areas have become fragmented by population movement, "Gentrification" etc. Local services are closer to hand and there is a greater variety of housing for sale. Transport links are also usually quite good and there are normally plenty of shops.

Disadvantages are less space, less privacy, more local activity, noise and pollution, less street parking, more expensive insurance and different schooling to rural environments. The incidence of crime and vandalism and levels of overall stress are higher in built-up urban areas. This is not the case with all built-up areas. It is up to the buyer to carry out research before making a commitment. If you are considering buying in a rural area, you might want to consider the following: there is more detached housing with land, more space and privacy. However, this can be undermined by the "village" syndrome where everyone knows your business, or wants to know your business. There is also cleaner air and insurance premiums can be lower. Disadvantages can be isolation, loneliness, lower level of services generally, and a limited choice of local education. One really good website which helps you compare all aspects of different areas is www.onefamily.com/best-places-live-work-uk.

Choosing your property

You should think carefully when considering purchasing a larger property. You may encounter higher costs, which may include:

- Larger, more expensive, carpeting
- More furniture. It is highly unlikely that your existing furniture will suit a new larger home.
- Larger gardens to tend. Although this may have been one of the attractions, large gardens are time consuming, expensive and hard work.
- Bigger bills
- More decorating
- Higher overall maintenance costs

Valuing a property

In the main, buyers will leave it to estate agents to offer a fair price, or market price for the house. If you want to compare estate agents valuations with others then you can access one of the websites, such as www.hometrack.com/uk or rightmove in order to gain a comparative value. Other sites are the Halifax, Nationwide, the Royal Institute of Chartered Surveyors, the National Association of Estate Agents and the Land Registry. You can also gain an idea of the valuation by looking in estate agents windows and assessing similar properties.

Purchasing a flat

There are some important points to remember when purchasing a flat. These are common points that are overlooked. If you purchase a flat in a block, the costs of maintenance of the flat will be your own. This is particularly pertinent now following the Grenfell tragedy and the problems with cladding on blocks of flats. Be very careful indeed when buying a flat. Important pieces of legislation to be aware of when deciding to buy a flat are the Building Safety Bill 2021 and the Fire Safety Act 2021. They deal with rights and responsibilities of Landlords and Tenants of leasehold properties and affect service charges and also future costs to leaseholders. There is also the government grant regime that deals with offsetting the costs of any future cladding related works. A lot of people are regretting deeply purchasing flats in high-rise blocks.

Of course, there are many flats that are not affected by the problems of cladding but be aware of any future obligations when buying a flat.

The costs of maintaining the common parts of blocks of flats will be down to the landlord (usually) paid for by you through a service charge. There has been an awful lot of trouble with service charges generally, apart from cladding issues. It has to be said that many landlords see service charges as a way of making profit over and above other income, such as ground rent, which is usually negligible after sale of a lease. However, see below concerning rising problems with ground rents as many unscrupulous developers have entered clauses in leases which cater for steep rise in ground rents, making flats virtually unsaleable.

Many landlords will own the companies that carry out the work and retain the profit made by these companies. They will charge leaseholders excessively for works which are often not needed. The 1996 Housing Act (as amended by the Commonhold and Leasehold Reform Act 2002) attempts to strengthen the hand of leaseholders against unscrupulous landlords by making it very difficult indeed for landlords to take legal action for forfeiture (repossession) of a lease without first giving the leaseholder a chance to challenge the service charges.

As mentioned above, be very careful if you are considering buying a flat in a block – you should establish levels of service charges and look at accounts. Try to elicit information from other leaseholders. It could be that there is a leaseholder's organisation, formed to manage their own service charges. This will give you direct control over contracts such as gardening, cleaning, maintenance contacts and cyclical decoration contracts. Better value for money is obtained in this way. In this case, at least you know that the levels will be fair, as no one leaseholder stands to profit.

It is important to know that under the Leasehold Reform Act 1993 as amended by the Commonhold and Leasehold Reform Act 2002 all leaseholders have the right to extend the length of their lease by a term of 90 years. For example, if your lease has 80 years left to run you can extend it to 170 Years. There is a procedure in the above Act for valuation. Leaseholders can also collectively purchase the freehold of the block. There is a procedure for doing this in the Act although it is often time consuming and can be expensive. There are advantages however, particularly when leaseholders are not satisfied with management.

In addition to service charges and length of lease, one other very important point is that of ground rents, as mentioned above. It has been reported widely in the press that many developers are setting ground rents (annual rents) far too high, and then selling off the freehold, which jeopardises the future saleability of the property. There have been a few court cases that have forced big developers such as Wimpy to make provision for compensation. The main tip here is make sure you look at the ground rent provisions when you buy, don't invest in something that can prove difficult to sell later on.

The problems with Airbnb from a point of view of a buyer of a flat
If you intend to reside in a home once purchased here are some tips to ensure that a flat you buy isn't in a block plagued by Airbnb guests:

- Read the lease. The lease should make it clear whether long term lets are viable or not. Although this does not always stop people sub-letting
- Talk to the concierge or porters-they will have a good idea of whether there are lots of short term guests and also whether or not there have been complaints
- Check Airbnb-if you are buying into a block then check the Airbnb site to see whether there are any up for let
- Find out who lives in the block and talk to them. Generally talking to other residents will give you an idea whether there are any problems with these short-term lets.

Remember the 90 day limit-are your neighbours breaking the rules? Residents, or potential residents should be aware that Airbnb has a 90 day limit per calendar year in London and a lot more local authorities are imposing this limit.

Airbnb says it will keep track of lettings and block the bookings of listings once the limit has been reached. However, as with everything, this can be abused by residents signing up to multiple agencies to enable them to let all year round.

Viewing properties

Before you start house hunting, draw up a list of characteristics you will need from your new home, such as the number of bedrooms, size of kitchen, garage, study and garden. Take the estate agents details with you when viewing. Also, take a tape measure with you. Assess the location of the property. Look at all the aspects and the surroundings. Give some thought as to the impact this will have in your future life. Assess the building, check the facing aspect of the property, i.e., north, south etc. and check the exterior carefully. Earlier, I talked about the need to be very careful when assessing a property. When you have made your mind up, a survey is essential.

If buying a house or ground floor flat, look for a damp proof course - normally about 15cm from the ground. Look for damp inside and out. Items like leaking rainwater pipes should be noted, as they can be a cause of damp. Look carefully at the windows. Are they rotten? Do they need replacing and so on. Look for any cracks. These should most certainly be investigated. A crack can be symptomatic of something worse or it can merely be surface. If you are not in a position to make this judgement then others should make it for you.

Heating is important. If the house or flat has central heating you will need to know when it was last tested. Gas central heating should be tested at least once a year. All in all you need to remember that you cannot see everything in a house, particularly on the first visit. A great deal may be being concealed from you. In addition, your own knowledge of property may be slim. A second opinion is a must.

Buying an old house

If you are considering purchasing an older house and making improvements then there are a number of things to think about: consider whether your proposed alterations will be in keeping with the age and style of the house, and neighbouring houses, particularly in a terrace. A classic mistake is that of replacing doors and windows with unsympathetic modern products. Again, salesmen will sell you anything and quite often won't provide the correct advice. If appropriate, you should consider contacting the Victorian Society victoriansociety.org.uk or the Georgian Group georgiangroup.org.uk for advice on preserving your home. Both offer leaflets to help you carry out appropriate restoration. It is often a good idea to employ an architect or surveyor to oversee any alterations you are considering. For local contractors contact the Royal Institute of British Architects or Royal Institute of Chartered Surveyors.

Renovation grants

These may be available from local authorities, although there are stringent requirements. They are means tested and the higher your income the more you are expected to pay. For further details you should contact your local authority direct.

Disabled facilities grant

A grant may be available to adapt a property for a disabled person, for example improving access into and around the home and adapting existing facilities within it. These grants are mandatory, but a discretionary grant is available to make a property suitable for the accommodation, welfare or employment of a disabled person. A leaflet, generally entitled Help for Disabled People with Adaptation and Other works, which can be obtained from your local authority, provides basic information.

Equalities Act 2010

The Equality Act 2010, with effect from October 2010, has introduced an obligation on all landlords to ensure that, if a disabled person requests it, suitable disabled access to common parts, and within common parts is available. Again, information is available from the local authority.

Planning permission

If you are considering alterations of a significant nature, either internal or external, you may need planning permission from your local authority. You may need planning permission if you plan to change the look or external aspect of the building or if you are intending to change the use.

You are allowed to carry out some work without planning permission, so it is worth contacting the local authority. You should also ask about building regulations. These are concerned with the materials and methods of building adopted. Regulations for work carried out in conservation areas are strict. The building control department at your local authority will be able to advise you about building regulations.

Buying a listed building

Buildings of architectural or historical interest are listed by the Secretary of State for National Heritage following consultation with English Heritage, to protect them against inappropriate alteration. In Wales, buildings are listed by the Secretary of State for Wales in consultation with CADW (Heritage Wales). In Scotland, they are listed by the Secretary of State for Scotland, in consultation with Historic Scotland. If you intend to carry out work to a listed building, you are likely to need listed building consent for any internal or external work, in addition to planning permission. The conservation officer in the local planning department can provide further information.

Buildings in conservation areas

Local authorities can designate areas of special architectural or historical significance. Conservation areas are protected to ensure that their character or interest is retained. Whole towns or villages may be conservation areas or simply one particular street. Strict regulations are laid down for conservation areas. Protection includes all buildings and all types of trees that are larger than 7cm across at 1.5m above the ground. There may be limitations for putting up signs, outbuilding or items such as satellite dishes. Any developments in the area usually have to meet strict criteria, such as the use of traditional or local materials.

This also applies to property in national parks, designated Areas of Outstanding Natural Beauty and the Norfolk or Suffolk Broads.

Whether or not a property is listed or is deemed to be in a conservation area will show up when your conveyancer carries out the local authority search.

Buying a new house or flat

There are a number of benefits to buying a new house or flat. You have the advantages of being the first occupants. There should not be a demand for too much maintenance or DIY jobs, as the building is new. There will, however, be a defects period which usually runs for 6 months for building and 12 months for electrical mechanical. During this period you should expect minor problems, such as cracking of walls, plumbing etc, which will be the responsibility of the builder.

One thing to note is that under the Building Safety Bill 2021, Leaseholders facing building safety remediation costs will be able to seek legal action for homes built up to 15 years ago.

Energy loss will be minimal. A new house or flat today uses 50 per cent less energy than a house built 15 years ago; consider the savings over an older property. An energy rating indicates how energy efficient a house is. The National House Building Council uses a rating scheme based on the National Energy Services Scheme, in which houses are giving a rating between 0 and 10. A house rated 10 will be very energy efficient and have very low running costs for its size. Security and safety are built in to new houses, smoke alarms are standard and security locks on doors and windows are usually included.

When the house market is slow developers usually offer incentives to buyers, such as cashback, payment of deposit etc. Sometimes they offer a part exchange scheme. These are definitely worth looking into. However, with part exchange you may not get the price you were looking for. One more important point: always check the tenure of the house-freehold or leasehold. Do try and avoid leasehold houses. The Government from 2018 onwards has banned the sale of any new leasehold houses, although some developers are trying to ignore the ban.

Building Guarantees

All new houses or flats should be built to certain standards and qualify for one of the building industry guarantees. These building guarantees are normally essential for you to obtain a mortgage and they also make the property attractive to purchasers when you move. A typical Guarantee is the National Housebuilding Council Guarantee (NHBC).

Housing plan lets buyers withhold payment until faults fixed

Ministers are preparing to allow buyers to withhold payments on shoddy new-built homes until all faults are repaired. Under the proposal first considered in 2020 by the housing and communities secretary, purchasers of all new homes could withhold from developers as much as 5 per cent of the sale price for up to six months. The final payment would be made only after the buyer was satisfied that all the faults in the property had been repaired. The move comes amid growing evidence of falling standards in the industry as home-builders try to meet government targets. The industry's figures show less than half of all buyers are satisfied with their new homes while 69 per cent reported five or more faults. Ministers are considering forcing building firms to publish satisfaction surveys, including the number of warranty claims for defects in their new houses.

Under the plan, which already operates in the Netherlands, a buyer's solicitor would retain a percentage of the purchase price for up to six months after completion. The money would be paid once all faults were fixed and could be subject to independent arbitration. There is no reason why it should not be extended to the private residential sector". The move follows fears in Whitehall that the government's drive to build up to 300,000 homes a year is coming at the expense of standards.

Websites for housebuilders

Most developers have their own websites with details and picture of their developments. These include both new properties and refurbished. In addition there are several websites that specialise in new properties only.

Buying a Rented House-Right to Buy

If you rent your house from your council, you will be able to buy it at a discount under Right-to-Buy legislation. The current government has increased discounts in an attempt to increase the right to buy. If you live in a new town, a housing association or housing association trust, you would need to make enquiries, as many are exempt, although the government announced that it was introducing legislation to force Housing Associations to sell properties under the right to buy. A compromise has been reached where this will be voluntary. The following rules apply to the Right to Buy:

- You get a 35% discount if you've been a public sector tenant for between 3 and 5 years.
- After 5 years, the discount goes up by 1% for every extra year you've been a public sector tenant, up to a maximum of 70% – or £82,800 across England and £110,500 in London boroughs (whichever is lower).

Flats
- You get a 50% discount if you've been a public sector tenant for between 3 and 5 years.
- After 5 years, the discount goes up by 2% for every extra year you've been a public sector tenant, up to a maximum of 70% – or £84,600 across England and £112,800 in London boroughs (whichever is lower).

If your landlord has spent money on your home

Your discount will be less if your landlord has spent money building or maintaining your home:

- in the last 10 years - if your landlord built or acquired your home before 2 April 2012
- in the last 15 years - if you're buying your home through Preserved Right to Buy, or if your landlord acquired your home after 2 April 2012

You won't get any discount if your landlord has spent more money than your home is now worth.

Social HomeBuy (shared ownership)

With Social HomeBuy, you buy a share of your council or housing association home and pay rent on the rest of it.

To apply, ask your landlord for an application form.

Discounts

You'll get a discount of between £9,000 and £16,000 on the value of your home, depending on:

- where your home is
- the size of the share you're buying

If you want to buy another share in your home later on, you'll get a discount on that too.

Buying more of your home later

You must buy at least 25% of your home. You can buy more later, until you own 100%. This is called 'staircasing'.

If you buy more of your home, your rent will go down - because it's based on how much of the property you rent. Your landlord can charge rent of up to 3% of the value of their share of your home, per year.

(see example overleaf)

ExampleYour home is worth £240,000 and you buy a 50% share. Your landlord charges you 3% rent on their 50% share. 3% of £120,000 is £3,600 per year. This works out at £300 per month for you to pay in rent.

Who can't apply

You can't use Social HomeBuy if:

- you have an assured shorthold tenancy
- you're being made bankrupt
- a court has ordered you to leave your home
- your landlord is taking action against you for rent arrears, anti-social behaviour or for breaking your tenancy agreement

Not all local councils or housing associations have joined the scheme. Check with your landlord to find out if they belong to the scheme and whether your home is included

Help to Buy Schemes

See chapter 4 for more details on Help to Buy and how it might benefit you.

Shared/part ownership property

There are properties available on a shared/part ownership basis, usually from housing associations. Local Authorities also provide such schemes, although rarely. The main principle is that you buy a percentage of the property, say 50% and you rent the rest, with a service charge if a flat. As time goes by, you can "staircase up" to

100% ownership. This is a scheme specially designed for those who cannot meet the full cost of outright purchase in the first instance. Usually, your total monthly outgoings are smaller than they would be if you purchased outright. Social Housing providers run a range of different schemes each year, largely depending on Government requirements. For further details you should contact a large housing association in your area who will provide you with current schemes on offer and point you in the right direction.

Self-build property

Self-build is another option for obtaining a new home. However, it is time consuming and not for the faint hearted. You need to be organised and to have organised the finances and your work programme. Usually the biggest problem is finding a suitable plot of land. There is a lot of competition. It also means that you will, unless you employ an agent, be charged with supervising a number of skilled craftsmen.

The Right to Build and Help to Build

These are two schemes introduced by the government which place an obligation on local authorities to assist people in finding land in their area (Right to Build) and also offer finance similar to Help to Buy. Details of these schemes can be found on the respective government websites www.gov.uk/government/right-to-build and www.ownyourhome.gov.uk/scheme/help-to-build.

Self-build usually works out cheaper than buying off a developer but it is certainly not an easy option. For more information and advice check out the following websites:

www.homebuilding.co.uk. This is run by the publishers of homebuilding and renovation magazine which is the leading magazine for homebuilders. The site is magazine style with lots of articles and also a link to www.plotfinder.net. This is a recently established database of land for sale and houses to renovate. There is an annual subscription cost, detailed on the website.

www.buildstore.co.uk

This site is owned by a group of venture capitalists, individuals and companies involved in the self build market. Again, there is a mix of articles and also adverts.

www.ebuild.co.uk

This site is published by specialist publisher's webguides on line. The site includes a directory of suppliers from architectural salvage to waste disposal with links to useful sites.

www.npbs.co.uk

This is the site of Norwich and Peterborough Building Society, who offer mortgages for self build projects. The loan for self-build is released in stages linked to the building of the property. It is worth checking to see if these mortgages are on offer.

****

Chapter 2

The Role of Estate Agents in Buying and Selling Property

Estate Agents

Estate agents are the normal route to buying or selling a home, although, as we will see later, online agents are offering cheaper deals for the sale or purchase of a property, many doing it for a fixed fee. Some of these agents however, such as Purple Bricks have run into trouble. Many people like the 'personal touch' and use agents. Agents generally have local knowledge and people on their books looking for specific types of property. However, there are things to watch out for, particularly in London, where there is a big demand and short supply. Estate agents will often try to charge various 'fees' for services and tie people into different charges in the contract. Always demand to know the fees and be sure where you are before you enter into a contract. A good site to get advice about estate agents fees is:

www.which.co.uk/money/mortgages-and-property/home-movers/selling-a-house/estate-agent-fees-and-contracts

What to expect from an estate agent:

- Advice on the selling or asking price of a house or flat - they know the local market
- Advice on the best way to sell (or buy) and where to advertise; they should discuss an advertising budget with you
- If selling, a meeting to visit, assess and value your home and also to take down the particulars of your home. The Property Misdescriptions Act 2010, which arose out of the bad old days of the 1980's, prevents agents from using ambiguous statements to enhance the sale of the property. You should look at the points carefully as people who are disappointed after reading such a glowing report will not purchase.
- They may ask for details of recent bills, such as council tax and electricity. They should also be willing to give advice on fixtures and fittings included in the sale.
- They should be willing to show potential buyers around your home if you are not available.
- Don't expect to have to pay for a for-sale board although some lenders will try to make a charge.

Although a seller does not have any specific duty to disclose information about a property, estate agents have specific legal obligations not to mislead members of the public.

Since 2014 agents have been covered by the general duties owed by other businesses to consumers that are set out in the

Consumer Protection from Unfair Trading Regulations 2008 as amended by the Consumer Protection (Amendment) Regulations 2014 (CPRs). These regulations include a ban on misleading statements or omissions and they effectively require estate agents to reveal any material facts about a property to potential buyers.

Choosing an agent if selling

Consider the following points:

- They ought to sell your type of property or specialise in one particular area of the market

- They should be a member of one of the professional bodies such as the National Association of Estate Agents, the Royal Institution of Chartered Surveyors, The Incorporated Society of Valuers and Auctioneers, The Architects and Surveyors Institute or the Association of Building Engineers.. Obtain quotes of fees, including the basic charge and any extras you might have to pay for, such as advertising in specialist publications.

Choose at least two agents to value the house, if instructing an agent.

Sole agency selling.

Offering an agent sole agency may reduce the fee. This can be done for a limited time. After this you can instruct multiple agents. With sole agency you can sell privately, although you may still be liable for the sole agent's fee.

Joint sole agents

With this arrangement, two or more agents co-operate in the house sale and split the commission. The agents may charge a higher commission in this case.

Multiple agency

This means that you have several agents trying to sell your home, but only pay the agent who sells your property.

Buying property using the internet-What is an online estate agent?

Online estate agents can help you sell your property without using a traditional high-street agent. Run via websites and call centres, they tend to offer a more basic service than you'd receive from a high-street agent and, as a result, they charge lower fees.

Two types of online agents have emerged over the last few years. Online-only estate agents require the seller to do most of the work themselves, from taking photos and creating an advert to handling buyer enquiries, conducting viewings and negotiating offers. But many online-only estate agents have now evolved into hybrid agencies, employing 'local property experts' to handle buyer enquiries, accompany viewings and negotiate offers.

How do online estate agents work?

The services offered by online estate agents - particularly hybrid agencies - are similar to those offered by high-street agents, but often in a more stripped-back form. Most online estate agents now offer the option of valuing and marketing your home and arranging property viewings. Many can also negotiate and accept offers on your behalf, and liaise with your conveyancer, other estate agents and buyers until the sale is complete. These services usually incur a higher fee than the basic service.

While high-street estate agents will usually charge you a percentage of your property's selling price, online estate agents generally charge fixed fees. This means that using an online agent is often much cheaper, especially if your home is worth a lot of money.

For example, if you sold a property worth £250,000 using a high-street estate agency that charged 1.3% commission, you'd pay £3,250. Online estate agents typically charge a flat fee of between £300 and £1,500, regardless of the value of your property.

A major downside of online estate agents' lower prices is that you'll often have to pay up front, regardless of whether they end up selling your home or not. Paying a fixed fee also reduces the agent's incentive to sell your property for the highest possible price. However, some online estate agents offer the option to pay once you've completed the sale but for a slightly higher price, reducing the risk of wasting your money. Some also offer a deferred payment option, where you pay at a defined point in the future, for example, 10 or 12 months down the line. This may involve entering into a credit agreement with the agency, so make sure you fully understand the terms before signing on the dotted line.

How are property valuations conducted?

An online-only agent is likely to use online data to value your home, while hybrid online estate agents will send a 'local expert' to provide a valuation. However, you won't necessarily get a valuer with specific knowledge of the local market. Remember you don't have to use the valuation provided. Ask several firms – high street or online – and go with an average, or whatever you think is the right price based on recent similar examples you've found through your own research. Inviting a variety of companies to value your home and talking to them about their sales process will also enable you to more deeply understand the differences between online and high street agents.

How will my property be marketed?

Online estate agents will list your home on their site as well as other online property portals such as Rightmove and Zoopla. Some will install a 'for sale' sign outside your house, although they might charge extra for this. High street estate agents will do all of the above as a standard part of their service, and can also place adverts in their branch windows.

How are viewings carried out?

The default option with most online estate agents is that you conduct the viewings yourself. However, a lot of online agents now offer accompanied viewings for an extra fee of around £300, or as part of a more expensive package than their standard offering.

Buyer vetting

Some (though not all) online estate agents will vet buyers, typically getting details of names, finances and whether potential buyers are already part of a chain.

How do I communicate with an online agent?

Someone will visit to take photographs and create floor plans if you sign up for this option, and you'll meet the 'local property expert' if the agency sends one round. However, all other contact will usually be via email or phone - and many online estate agencies offer online portals where you can access helplines or chat services outside traditional working hours, with some offering 24/7 support.

What are my rights when using an online estate agent?

Online estate agents are governed by the same regulations that cover high street estate agents.As with high street agents, online estate agents must be members of a government-approved redress scheme – the Property Ombudsman Limited or the Property Redress Scheme. Your agent has to be clear about which redress scheme they are a member of, and the scheme should be your first port of call if you have a problem.Trading Standards will also investigate agents that it believes have acted in breach of the 1979 Estate Agent Act, which sets out minimum standards of conduct for estate agents. They are also governed by The Consumer Protection from Unfair Trading Regulations 2008.

Pros and cons of online estate agents

Online estate agents can be a great money-saving option when you're selling your house, but you should be aware of the pros and cons of these services before making a decision. Pros of using an online estate agent:

- Fees: in most cases, using an online estate agent will be a lot cheaper than using a high-street agent. The more expensive your home is, the more you stand to save if they charge a flat fee.

- Convenience: it can sometimes be easier to get hold of online estate agents. Their call centres are open during evenings and weekends, so they are able to deal with queries outside of working hours (although some high-street agents offer this, too).

- Flexibility: packages can be tailored to your specific requirements, and you can often track viewings and feedback online (some high-street agents also offer this).

- Freedom to use multiple agents: generally, there is no contract period, which means you can instruct other estate agents if you wish.

Cons of using an online estate agent

- Lack of local knowledge: even online agents with regional reps could struggle to compete with a high-street agent who knows your neighbourhood and its property market inside out.
- Legwork: some online estate agents won't negotiate offers or act as a middleman to progress your sale to completion. Having to manage communications with buyers and solicitors on your own can be time-consuming and stressful.
- Viewings: you usually have to conduct viewings yourself, so you'll need to be comfortable showing strangers around your home and be available during evenings and weekends.
- Paying up front: if you opt for this type of package, you won't be paying on results. In fact, you'll have to pay even if that company doesn't end up selling your house.
- Selling price: because most online estate agents charge a flat fee rather than commission, they have less incentive to get the best price for you. That said, they have reputations to maintain, and many companies claim they usually achieve the asking price.

As stated, there are a number of websites that also detail properties, some are independent and some are owned by the large players. The following are a selection of the main sites:

www.rightmove.co.uk.

This is one of the largest sites, jointly owned and run by Halifax, Royal Sun Alliance, Connell and Countryside assured Group. They jointly claim to represent more than 170,000 properties covering 99% of UK postcodes. The main function of this site is as a property search site, enabling people to search for property by name of area and postcode. Each property has a reference number and will have a photo and details. These can be obtained by clicking on the property. There is much useful information, including room sizes.

www.zoopla.co.uk

The claims of this website are that it can help the buyer to find a property, move home and settle in.

www.primelocation.co.uk

This site was launched in 2000 by a consortium of estate agents. This site deals with more expensive properties.

Selling property using the internet

Although estate agents are still the main avenues for selling property, as we have seen, the web now plays a more significant part. In addition to the websites detailed, almost all agents now have their own website. This is really an electronic shop window where your property is displayed. Buyers interested in your property should be able to e-mail the estate agent directly for a viewing.

Ten top tips when selling a property

If you are selling a property, there are a number of things that you need to get right in order to ensure the best chance on the market:

- Get the price right-this is absolutely crucial-if you try to overprice then you will harm your chances of a sale as you will lose the trust of would-be purchasers-pitch the price attractively.

- Make your property presentable-remember that you are selling your home and you should show it to its best advantage.

- get the photos right

- make sure it is described fully-do not mss anything out.

- make your agent work for you. the first 30 days on the property market are crucial. make sure you are in regular contact with

- them.

- Don't forget to include a floor plan.

- make sure you have all the relevant certificates and paperwork, such as gas and electricity certificates, and damp proofing etc.

This advice applies whether you are using a traditional high street agent or are using an online agent. make sure that what you are selling is shown in its best light.

****

Chapter 3

Buying a Property-The Practicalities

___

Considerations when buying a house or flat

How to speed up a house sale

The government is considering introducing a reservation agreement, which legally commits both parties to the sale, to try to curb the third of sales that collapse each year. This type of agreement already exists in Scotland, where accepted offers become legally binding after a series of negotiations known as missives.

In England and Wales the government has been working on a standardised reservation agreement that would involve buyers and sellers paying either a flat fee or a percentage of the purchase price into a central pot. Whoever is at fault for a sale falling through would be held liable, subject to some exemptions. The system is being discussed by focus groups to decide whether to trial it with estate agencies. The chief executive of Rightmove, an online property site, says an agreement would provide more information up-front and reduce delays. Reservation agreements are already common when buying new-builds. London-based estate agencies have offered reservation agreements for its new-build business for some time, but are now extending it to other property sales. Typically, agencies ask for a £2,000 reservation agreement deposit from buyers for properties valued at less than £1 million and £5,000 for those worth more. This comes off the price when the sale completes, but agencies say it shows the buyer is serious and speeds up sales. Other companies who offer this service include:

Gazeal

Gazeal is company that is trying to speed up and protect sales by getting sellers to provide property and legal information through a conveyancer at the listing stage, so a potential buyer has more details before making an offer. Once an offer is made, Gazeal requires a buyer to pay a non-refundable fee of 0.075 per cent of the agreed purchase price for a reservation deposit guarantee. If they pull out of the transaction price. Gazeal will pay this to the seller and chase the buyer for the debt. The seller is also committed to paying 1 per cent of the transaction if they withdraw. Both parties also pay £250 on completion of transaction. There is a 14-day cooling-off period, or 21 days if a buyer needs time to apply for a mortgage, before the agreement is signed. This provides time for a survey or valuation to raise any issues, and it can be extended if necessary, agreed by both parties.

Honesty Box

Honesty Box lets buyers and sellers guarantee a transaction by committing a deposit of either £500 or £1,000 each. Users can choose an absolute lock, which won't allow anyone to back out. or a qualified lock that stipulates certain circumstances where either party can exit. If the sale completes, the buyer and seller get their deposit back minus a fee of £75 for a £500 deposit, and £150 for a £1,000 deposit. A buyer will lose their money if they pull out and it will be given to the seller, and vice versa if the vendor withdraws.

Pre-Contract Deposit

Pre-Contract Deposit charges £245 plus VAT to set up a reservation agreement between a buyer and seller. Both parties pay a deposit of 1 per cent of the purchase price, which is refunded when the sale completes,

Pre-Contract Deposit investigates and whoever is at fault has to pay 25 per cent of their deposit to the other party. Both sides will get their deposit back if it is decided that no one is to blame.

The downsides

Buyers and sellers may be put off by the extra paperwork and costs involved in arranging a reservation agreement. They are only available if an agency is signed up to one of the above services. You can search for agencies that offer these agreements through a provider's website or you could ask it to join. Also there may be issues if a buyer or seller refuses to take the blame for a fall-through, but all the services offer arbitration to resolve disputes.

Budgeting

Before beginning to look for a house you need to sit down and give careful thought to the costs involved in the whole process. The starting point is to identify the different elements in the overall transaction.

Deposits

Sometimes the estate agent will ask you for a small deposit when you make the offer (see Estate Agents, chapter 2). This indicates that you are serious about the offer and is a widespread and legitimate practice, as long as the deposit is not too much, £100 is usual. The main deposit for the property, i.e., the difference between the mortgage and what has been accepted for the property, isn't paid until the exchange of contracts. Once you have exchanged contracts on a property the purchase is legally binding. Until then, you are free to withdraw. The deposit cannot be reclaimed after exchange. The main rule of thumb is that less you borrow the more favourable terms you can normally get from bank or building society. Banks have tightened up their lending criteria considerably. The Mortgage Market review came into effect in 2014 which imposed further restrictions on banks and building society lending and requires a stringent set of checks carried out before a mortgage is approved. All lenders insist on larger minimum deposits. This will vary with the bank or building society and you should also scan the Sunday newspapers in particular for details of best buys for mortgages. Refer to chapter 4 for details on help to buy, with the government guaranteeing deposits.

Stamp duty- What is stamp duty and who pays it?

Stamp Duty — Stamp Duty Land Tax (SDLT) official jargon-is a tax you pay when you buy a home. The buyer pays stamp duty– not the person selling. Stamp duty applies to both freehold and leasehold purchases over £125,000

First-time buyers pay no tax on homes costing up to £500,000. Second-home owners continue to pay 3% on values above £40,000.

Property Price	SDLT Rate
Up to £125,000	0%
Over £125,000 and under £250,000	2%
Over £250,000 and under £925,000	5%
Over £925,000 and under £1,500,000	10%
Over £1,500,000	12%

For more details of the various stamp duty rates go to: https://www.gov.uk/stamp-duty-land-tax note that stamp duty land tax is different in Scotland.

Buying off plan-beware of SDLT costs

Anyone buying a new home off-plan could be hit with a tax bill for tens of thousands of pounds after a court ruling in 2019. Desmond Higgins put down a deposit on a two-bedroom flat in the former St Pancras Station Hotel, London, in 2004, but could not move in until 2010 because of construction delays. When he sold it two years after moving in, HM Revenue & Customs (HMRC) handed him a capital gains tax (CGT) bill of £61,383, which included the gain made between 2004 and 2010, when the flat had not been built. The taxman argued that Higgins was not eligible for private residence relief, which is usually given to someone selling their main residence, because he had not lived in the property until 2010, Higgins said that he could not live in the property because it did not exist. He had been forced to find temporary accommodation during the delays, so there was no way that the St Pancras property could be classed as a second home for tax purposes. The Upper Tribunal ruled in HMRC's favour, charging Higgins the five-figure bill. Experts say the ruling is baffling and could have wide tax implications for buyers suffering construction delays, which could become more common during the economic slowdown. They also suggest that it is a stealthy attempt by the taxman to cash in on the rapid appreciation of property prices. Between 2000 and 2010, the average property price in London more than doubled, rising from £164,000 to £385,000.

HMRC says that most of those who buy off-plan will still be eligible for Extra-Statutory Concession D49, which allows up to two years for building work to be completed before you move in without any loss of private residence relief. However, anyone affected by construction delays longer than this will face charges. HMRC says it calculated Higgins CGT calculation as if he had owned the property in full from 2006 when he exchanged contracts; he was granted a lease in 2007, but paid the full balance only upon completion of the purchase on January 5, 2010.

Beat the stamp duty surcharge

It should be noted that homebuyers could claim back from the taxman after a legal ruling in 2019 found that uninhabitable properties should not be liable for the stamp duty surcharge on second homes. The extra 3 per cent has been imposed since April 2016 on properties bought in addition to buyer's main home. A tax tribunal heard in Bristol this month found in favour of Paul and Nikki Bewley, who bought a derelict bungalow in Weston-super-Mare for £200,000 as a buy-to-let investment in January 2017. It was riddled with asbestos and had no central heating. The couple demolished it and built a new home its place. HM Revenue & Customs (HMRC) argued that a buyer should be liable for the higher rate of stamp duty if a property was capable of being used as a dwelling in the future, but the tribunal disagreed, saying that the charge should be levied only if the home was suitable for immediate habitation. Experts say that the case could open the door for hundreds of claims from buy-to-let investors who paid the additional charge for the purchase of properties that needed renovation.

The Bewleys, who represented themselves in court, paid the normal rate of £1,500 in stamp duty when they bought the house but were later told by HMRC they should have paid £7,500, including the surcharge. According to the Housing Acts a property must have lavatory, cooking and bathing facilities to be considered habitable. However, what constitutes a dilapidated home will now be the subject of a bitter legal battle.

Other costs

A solicitor normally carries out conveyancing of property. However, it is perfectly normal for individuals to do their own conveyancing. All the necessary paperwork can be obtained from legal stationers and it is executed on a step-by-step basis. It has to be said that solicitors are now very competitive with their charges and, for the sake of between £600-£900, it is better to let someone else do the work which allows you to concentrate on other things.

Land Registry

The Land Registry records all purchases of land in England and Wales and is open to the public (inspection of records, called a property search). The registered title to any particular piece of land or property will carry with it a description and include the name of owner, mortgage, rights over other persons land and any other rights. There is a small charge for inspection. A lot of solicitors have direct links and can carry out searches very quickly. Not all properties are registered although it is now a duty to register all transactions. (See chapter 6, conveyancing)

Energy Performance Certificates (EPC's)

EPC's are compulsory and there is now more attention than ever on the energy performance of houses, particularly after the conference on climate change in 2021 and the government's commitment to reduce our carbon footprint.

An EPC surveyor will assess the property and looks at all the ways a house or flat can waste heat, such as inadequate loft insulation, lack of cavity wall insulation, draughts and obsolete boilers. After the assessment they will award a rating from A (as good as it gets) to G (terrible). The document also includes information and advice on how to improve matters, such as lagging the water tank or installing double-glazing.

An EPC will cost between £75-£130 (although they can be cheaper if you shop around online) and will be valid for ten years. Improvements made while the certificate is in force will not need a new survey. Watch out for companies that offer them for higher prices. Always search around.

Structural surveys

The basic structural survey is the homebuyers survey and valuation which is normally carried out by the building society or other lender. This will cost you between £250-£500 and is not really an in-depth survey, merely allowing the lender to see whether they should lend or not, and how much they should lend. Sometimes, lenders keep what they refer to as a retention, which means that they will not forward the full value (less deposit) until certain defined works have been carried out. If you want to go further than a homebuyers report then you will have to instruct a firm of surveyors who have several survey types, depending on how far you want to go and how much you want to spend.

A word of caution. Many people go rushing headlong into buying a flat or house. They are usually exhilarated and wish to complete their purchase fairly quickly in order to establish their new home. If you stop and think about this, it is complete folly and can prove very expensive later. A house or flat is a commodity, like other commodities, except that it is usually a lot more expensive. A lot can be wrong with the commodity that you have purchased which is not immediately obvious. Only after you have completed the deal and paid over the odds for your purchase do you begin to regret what you have done.

The true price of a property is not what the estate agent is asking, certainly not what the seller is asking. The true market price is the difference between what a property in good condition is being sold at and your property minus cost of works to bring it up to that value. Therefore, if you have any doubts whatsoever, and if you can afford it get a detailed survey of the property you are proposing to buy and get the works required costed out. When negotiating, this survey is an essential tool in order to arrive at an accurate and fair price. Do not rest faith in others, particularly when you alone stand to lose. One further word of caution. As stated, a lot of problems with property cannot be seen. A structural survey will highlight those. In some cases it may not be wise to proceed at all.

Mortgage fees-Mortgage indemnity insurance.

This is a one-off payment if you are arranging a mortgage over 70-80% of lenders valuation. This represents insurance taken out by the lender in case the purchaser defaults on payments, in which case the lender will sell the property to reclaim the loan. It is to protect the mortgage lender not the buyer. The cost of the insurance varies depending on how much you borrow. A 90% mortgage on a £60,000 property will cost between £300-600. For a 100% mortgage it is usually much higher. You have to ask yourself, if you are paying up to £2,000 for this kind of insurance on a 100% mortgage, is it not better to try to raise the money to put down a bigger deposit.

Always think about the relative economics. A lot of money is made by a lot of people in house buying and selling. The loser is usually the buyer or seller, not the host of middlemen. So think carefully about what you are doing.

Mortgage arrangement fees

Depending upon the type of mortgage you are considering you may have to pay an arrangement fee.

Buildings insurance

When you have purchased your property you will need to take out buildings insurance. This covers the cost of rebuilding your home if it is damaged. It also covers the cost of subsidence, storm and flood damage, burst pipes and other water leaks and vandalism and third party damage generally. The insurance company will tell you more about elements covered. It is worth shopping around for buildings insurance as prices vary significantly. Many banks/building societies also supply buildings insurance if you arrange a mortgage with them. You shouldn't immediately take up their offer, as they are not always the most competitive. Websites such as www.confused.com can provide a range of quotes for you.

Removals

Unless you are not moving far and are considering doing it yourself, you should budget for hiring a removal firm. This will depend on how many possessions you have and how much time and money you have. Take care when choosing the removal firm. Choose one who comes recommended if possible. There are other costs too. Reconnection of telephone lines and possibly a deposit, carpets, curtains and plumbing-in washing machines. How much you pay will probably depend on how handy you are yourself. There are also smaller incidental costs such as redirecting mail by the post office. We will be discussing moving home in more depth later on in chapter 8.

Costs of moving

The table below will give you an idea of typical costs, such as solicitors fees, stamp duty, land registry fees and search fees when buying a property. The costs are based on a purchase of a typical London property (not first time buyer). Other costs as discussed above will be extra. It has to be stressed that, apart from the stamp duty and Land Registry Fees (which should be checked as below is for guidance only) solicitor's costs and searches will vary. Searches will cost more in different areas and solicitors fees will come down.

House price	Solicitors fees (av)	Stamp duty	Land Registry	Search fees	Total fees £
£150,000	£900	£500	200	200	*1800*
£200,000	£1,000	£1500	200	200	2900
£300,000	£1000	5000	280	235	6,515
£500,000	£1000	£15,000	280	280	16,560
£750,000	1069	27,500	280	280	29129
£1m	1372	43,750	920	235	46277
£1.5m	1895	£93,750	920	235	96800
£2m	2208	£153750	920	235	157313
£2.5m	2723	£213750	920	235	217628
£3m	3656	273750	920	235	278561
£3.5m	4231	£333750	920	235	339135
£4m	4871	393750	920	235	399776

The process of buying a property

Having considered the basic elements of buying a property, the next step is to find the property you want. As we have discussed, this is a long and sometimes dispiriting process. Trudging around estate agents, sorting through mountains of literature, dealing with mountains of estate agents details, scouring the papers and walking the streets! However, most of us find the property we want at the end of the day. It is then that we can put in our offer. One useful way of determining the respective values of property in different areas is to visit a website set up for that purpose www.hometrack.co.uk. This particular site collects price information from selected estate agents in different postcode areas across the country. Before you decide to look, a little research into prices and comparisons with what you can afford might be useful.

Making an offer

You should put your offer in to the estate agent or direct to the seller, depending who you are buying from. As discussed earlier, your offer should be based on sound judgement, on what the property is worth not on your desire to secure the property at any cost. A survey will help you to arrive at a schedule of works and cost. If you cannot afford to employ a surveyor from a high street firm then you should try to enlist other help. In addition, you should take a long and careful look at the house yourself, not just a cursory glance. Look at everything and try to get an idea of the likely cost to you of rectifying defects. However, I cannot stress enough the importance of getting a detailed survey. Eventually, you will be in a position to make an offer for the property.

You should base this offer on sound judgement and you should provide a rationalisation for your offer, if it is considerably lower than the asking price. You should make it clear that your offer is subject to contract and survey (if you require further examination or wish to carry out a survey after the offer).

Putting your own home on the market

Most people moving try to secure the sale of their own home before looking for a new one. If you haven't started to sell your house yet, you are advised to do so as soon as possible. You need also to arrange finance. A lot of people have had the nightmarish experience of stepping into an estate agents and being besieged by "independent" financial advisors wishing to sell you their product. Be very careful at this stage. See "getting your mortgage" chapter 5.

Exchange of contracts

Once the buyer and seller are happy with all the details stated in the contract and your conveyancer can confirm that there are no outstanding legal queries, those conveyancing will exchange contracts. The sale is now legally binding for both parties. You should arrange the necessary insurances, buildings and contents from this moment on as you are now responsible for the property.

Buying with a friend

The 1996 Family Law Act brought in the concept of cohabiting couples having the same rights as married couples. This will apply particularly if your marriage starts to break up and you wish to ascertain property rights. However, it is wise to draw up a cohabitation contract prior to purchase which will put in writing how the property is shared and will make clear the situation after break-up. The cohabitation contract can include any conditions you wish and is drawn up usually by a solicitor. There are standard forms for cohabitation agreements which can include financial arrangements stating who pays for the mortgage, who can call for a sale, mutual wills, and who pays for and owns possessions. You can obtain a leaflet concerning this from a Citizens Advice Bureau or from a solicitor.

Completing a sale

This is the final day of the sale and normally takes place around ten days after Exchange. Exchange and completion can take place on the same day if necessary but this is unusual.

On day of completion, you are entitled to vacant possession and will receive the keys. See chapter 6 for more details on the conveyancing process.

Buying at auction

Although many people will go through the traditional route of acquiring property through an estate agent, there are other routes, one main one being the auction. Buying at auction requires a different set of skills and you need to know what you are buying, where it is and what the problems are, if any.

Why is it being sold at auction? Certainly, you need to act fairly quickly as you need to inspect the property before auction day, arrive at the final bid price that you will not exceed and be prepared to complete within 28 days.

What is a property auction?

The process is very similar to the normal method of private sale. However, for an auction sale the seller and their solicitor carry out all the necessary paperwork and legal investigations prior to the auction. Subject to the property receiving an acceptable bid, the property will be 'sold' on auction day with a legally binding exchange of contracts and a fixed completion date.

Different types of property auction houses

Auction houses vary in size and the amount of business that they conduct and the frequency with which they hold auctions. Most will sell both residential and commercial property and each will have its own style of operation, and fee structure. Large auction houses will hold auctions frequently, perhaps every two months and will have around 250 lots for sale. A lot of the auctions happen in London. Most of the large auction houses will deal with property put forward by large institutions, such as banks selling repossessions.

Also local authorities and will advertise the sales in the mainstream media and trade papers. The medium size auction houses will hold auctions as frequently as they can, in regional venues, such as racecourses and conference centres, and depending on stock, usually every two to three months, tending to advertise locally. The small auction houses will have far fewer lots and will hold their sales in smaller local venues. They may advertise in local press but more often will trade on word of mouth.

Those who attend auctions

As you might imagine, all sorts of people attend auctions. The common denominator is that they are all interested in buying property.

Property investors are most common at auction, people who are starting out building a portfolio or those who have large portfolios that they wish to expand. They tend to fall into two groups, those who are after capital appreciation, i.e. buy at a low value and build the capital value and those who are looking for rental income. Then there are the property traders who like a quick profit from buying and 'flipping' property. These types usually have intimate knowledge of an area and are well placed to make a quick profit. Then we have the developers who look for small profitable sites or larger sites where property can be built and sold on. The sites can have existing buildings on them or can be vacant lots with or without planning permission. Last, but not least, we have those people who intend to buy solely for the purpose of owner occupation, look to buy a below- value property that they can redesign and make their own.

What types of property are suitable for auction?

There is strong demand for all types of properties offered at auction. These may be properties requiring updating, those with short leases, development sites with or without planning permission, repossessions, forced sales and, investment properties. Also ground rents, probates, receivership sales and local authority properties. However, any type of property can be sold at auction and initially the property will be inspected to discuss specific criteria and the current situation. Extensive research will be carried out by the auction house and advice offered as to whether auction is the appropriate method of sale.

Why is property being sold at an auction?

There are a number of reasons why property is sold at an auction:

- A quick sale is needed, often due to the owner being in financial difficulties or it is a repossession
- There are structural problems which prevent the property being sold easily in the conventional manner.
- Properties sold by public bodies. Here you get all sort of property, including weird and wonderful properties such as

public toilets and police stations, all of which may have their uses.

- The property is unique and there are no direct comparisons, such as lighthouses and the above-mentioned public toilet.

It is always best to find out why exactly the property is being sold at auction. Is it so difficult to get rid of because of some inherent reason? Ask why is this property at auction and not being sold in the conventional way? Who exactly is the vendor and what if any are the problems stopping it being sold conventionally? The reasons that the property is at auction may be entirely innocent but it is always worth finding out to avoid future problems.

What happens next?

Once you have found your auction, to receive a complimentary auction catalogue you should contact the Auctioneers and this will give the information about the properties being offered for sale. You can also download a catalogue from the auctioneers website. The catalogue includes descriptions of the available properties, legal information, viewing arrangements and a guide price, which is purely an indication of a realistic selling price. This should not be taken as a firm asking or selling price and should be relied upon as a guide only. Professional advice must be taken in relation to any lot in which there is an interest.

For lots where viewings are arranged, these are carried out on a block basis and are published in all advertising and in the auction catalogue. Any prospective purchaser is welcome at these viewings and should the scheduled appointments be inconvenient, alternative arrangements can be made. Any interest must be registered with the Auctioneers in order that prospective purchasers may be kept informed as to the progress of the sale.

Bidding for a property

The lots will be offered and the bidding taken to the highest possible level and once the gavel falls, the contracts will be exchanged. The buyer purchases the property at the price they bid - this cannot be negotiated and the stipulated terms cannot be changed. The buyer will then pay 10% of the purchase price on the day and completion occur 28 days later. The funds are then paid to the seller less the fees of the Auctioneers and those of the seller's solicitor.

The atmosphere of an auction room can be extremely exciting and competitive and it is often the case that an interested party will bid in excess of the figure that had previously been set as their maximum. In some cases, the prices achieved at auction can be higher than those achieved by private treaty.

The seller will provide a legal pack that may be inspected at any time. Auctioneers will strongly advise that professional advice is obtained from a legal representative. Details of the seller's solicitors will be available and, should a mortgage be required, it is advisable to have this in place prior to the sale. Again, Auctioneers strongly advise that funding is discussed with a professional advisor prior to attending the sale.

The successful buyer will be required to pay 10% of the purchase price on the day, together with a buyer's premium which is normally £250 including VAT. The balance of the purchase price is required on the agreed completion day and this is normally 28 days after the auction, however this can vary so best to check with the auction house.

Bidding from your smart phone

A new e'Bay for home buyers' is already big business making it easy to bid and buy via smartphone

Homeowners wary of the auction room when it comes to buying or selling might prefer a new digital online auction called BidX1 (bidx1.com). It is a bit like online goods market eBay but for property – and the latest sale is today.

Difficulties of raising finance, bargains that turn into bottomless pits, fears about losing deposits, overbidding, and auctioneers plucking "2 bids off the wall" still put many off the traditional "ballroom" auction. But BidX1, up and running in the UK for 18 months, could be modifying that image. Most significant is the holding of a £4,500 "buyers fee" at registration to enable you to bid. If you win with the highest bid, you must pay a 10 per cent deposit at once and complete the purchase in 20 business days, possibly extended if over Christmas. Each time a highest bid is made, the auction automatically extends for a further minute and only closes when there are no further bids. BidX1's registration system for buyers and sellers complies with UK money laundering regulations and enables both sides to see on-screen who is bidding, how much, and when. BidX1's system can also see where the bid is from geographically and on what sort of device it was made. Customers can view, bid, buy and sell from home on a mobile phone. And it seems the detailed knowledge and visibility of who is bidding what, is of interest to both residential and commercial buyers and sellers because records can be checked. BidX1's fees are one-and-a- half to two-and-a half per cent of the sale price, depending on the sale and complexity of what's offered.

How do prospective purchasers find out legal and survey information for the properties in which they are interested?
A legal pack is requested from each of the vendor's solicitors and this contains copies of all legal papers, which will be required by any prospective purchasers for them to make an informed decision regarding the purchase of any lot. The pack will include office copy entries and plans, the relevant local authority search, leases (if applicable), Special Conditions of Sale, replies to pre-contract enquiries and any other relevant documents. A copy of these legal packs can usually be obtained from auctioneers for a small charge. Should any additional information be required, the seller's solicitors

are listed in the catalogue and can be contacted directly. All legal packs are available for inspection at each auction.

Any purchase at auction takes place under the assumption that documentation and the terms of the contract have been read.

It is strongly recommended that any potential purchasers carry out full investigations for any lot in which they have an interest and a survey is an integral part of that investigation.

How is finance arranged?

Should a mortgage be required, approval in principle must be obtained prior to auction. Lenders are now familiar with the auction process and are usually willing to provide a mortgage offer for buyers intending to purchase at auction. A valuation and survey will be required along with legal evidence that there are no issues that will affect the value.

It is essential that the lender can provide funds within the timescale for completion. On the day of the auction, the purchaser will need to pay 10% of the purchase price and must ensure there are cleared funds to pay this amount. Sometimes, finance can be arranged through an auctioneers on request.

Can lots be bought before auction?

Vendors may consider offers submitted before auction day. Any such offers need to be submitted in writing to an auctioneers - this will be referred to the vendor and their instruction will be passed on to the prospective purchaser. Offers will have to be unconditional and the buyer must be in a position to exchange contracts and pay the required deposit before auction day. no offers are considered within five days of the auction.

House swapping

House swapping is an unorthodox but cost effective way of obtaining the property that you are looking for. It is a very efficient way of buying a property. Essentially, you find the property that you want and the seller moves into your house. There is no chain because you are cutting out other buyers. Obviously, the biggest problem is finding someone that you want to swap with and who wants to swap with you.

In practice, the estate agent should be the ideal key player in any swap arrangement. They have a large number of people on their books and who have provided details of their requirements. However, this way of operating seems to be beyond all but the most enterprising estate agencies. In practice, most swaps happen through coincidence.

Saving money through swapping homes

There is a significant saving to be made by swapping homes. If you are the one trading down, for example you have a home worth £275,000 and you want to swap it for a flat worth £150,000, the owner of the flat will be paying for your house with part cash part property. As far as HMRC is concerned this is not a sale on which you would pay stamp duty, but a transfer on which you would pay a notional sum of just £5. However, in this particular type of transaction solicitors must draw up the deal as a single contract with the more expensive property paid partly in kind and partly in cash. You can also save on estate agents fees if you find your swap independently. A useful website dealing with home swaps is:

www.home-swap.org.uk. Registration on the site is free.

****

Chapter 4

More about Mortgages

_____

Most people purchasing a property will need a mortgage. There are many products on the market and deposits are not always required. However, it is crucial that you are in possession of all the facts when making a decision about a mortgage.

Financial advisers will give you plenty of advice but not always the best advice. Sometimes it is better to go to the lender direct. Before you talk to lenders, work out what your priorities are, such as tax advantage, early repayment and so on. Make sure that you are aware of the costs of life cover.

Lenders-Banks and building societies

There is little or no difference between the mortgages offered by banks and building societies. Because banks borrow against the wholesale money markets, the interest rate they charge to borrowers will fluctuate (unless fixed) as and when their base rate changes. Building societies however, will rely more heavily on their savers deposits to fund their lending and may adjust the interest rate charged for variable mortgages only once a year. This may be a benefit or disadvantage, depending on whether rates are going up or down.

Centralised lenders

Centralised lenders borrow from the money markets to fund their lending and have no need for the branch network operated by banks and building societies. Centralised lenders, which came to the fore during the 1980s, particularly the house price boom, have been criticised for being quick to implement increases but slow to implement decreases, through rate reductions. This is, simply, because they exist to make profit. Therefore, you should be cautious indeed before embarking on a mortgage with lenders of this kind.

Brokers and "independent" financial advisors

Brokers act as intermediaries between potential borrowers and mortgage providers. If they are "tied" agents they can only advise on the products of one bank, insurance company or building society. If they are independent they should, technically, advise and recommend on every product in the market place.

A word of warning. It is up to you to ask detailed questions about any product a broker offers you. Since 2013, advisors have to charge a fee and advertise this fee. Prior to this they charged a commission, the costs of which fell onto the borrower. Many brokers sell unsuitable products because they receive healthy commissions. In the 1980s it became impossible to enter an estate agents office without being forced to enter into discussions with financial advisers who were intent on selling you products which made them a lot of money. If possible, you should arrange a mortgage direct with a bank and avoid so called independent brokers.

How much can you borrow?

At the time of writing, 2022, the Bank of England is looking to loosen the stringent finance checks to enable lenders to lend more. Traditionally, there is a standard calculation for working out the maximum mortgage that you will be allowed. For one borrower, three times annual salary, for a joint mortgage, two or two and a half times combined. Lenders, however, will vary and some will lend more. Be very careful not to overstretch yourself. As stated, banks and building societies have tightened up their lending criteria and mortgages are hard to obtain without hefty deposits. The Financial Conduct Authority has introduced tough new rules to ensure that no one can borrow more than they can afford to repay. Under the current rules, interest only mortgages will only be offered to people with a firm and clear repayment plan, rather than simply relying on the rise in house prices to cover repayment of the capital. Lenders will also have to take account of future interest rate increases on repayment costs.

After the 2008 credit crunch and the financial crash that followed, the UK government carried out a thorough review of the mortgage market, implementing changes that came into force in 2014.

These changes were the result of the conclusion drawn by the government that mortgages were too readily available too many high-risk mortgages had been approved, ones where borrowers couldn't make their repayment, and this had exacerbated the crash. To avoid this happening again, the government decided to tighten lending requirements for mortgages, which is where the mortgage market review, or MMR, comes in. It was one of the most significant changes ever made to the UK mortgage market and had a considerable impact on both lenders and borrowers.

What Is The MMR?

In essence, the MMR is an assessment of affordability. It requires all lenders to carry out stress tests to make sure a borrower can make their mortgage repayments even if interest rates rise. As part of this stress test, borrowers need to provide evidence of their ability to repay their mortgage including having stable and sufficient sources of income and limited borrowings.

What Is Included In The Affordability Assessment?

Previously, lenders had made decisions based on a person's income, calculating how much they could borrow by multiplying their salary. Now, they must make a more detailed assessment of a borrower's overall financial situation that includes:

- **Your credit report and credit score**
- Your employment history and income

- Your account balance over a set period, flagging any unusual deposits, income or outgoings (which you might need to explain)
- Whether you have savings, and if you save regularly
- Whether you live within your means or carry an overdraft
- How you spend your money, e.g. do you gamble excessively or take expensive holidays Regular outgoings, e.g. rent, child care, memberships or school fees
- Other credit commitments, e.g. loans, credit cards, hire purchase agreements or other regular outgoings, e.g. Netflix.

The bank can do this assessment, or they may use the services of an underwriter to decide on whether you are approved for a mortgage.

Interest-Only Mortgages

The MMR also brought about changes that restricted the availability of interest-only mortgages, which require the borrower to pay back the capital costs at the end of the mortgage term. Borrowers wanting an interest-only mortgage must now provide detailed financial plans evidencing how they will make payments.

The Impact On Existing Mortgage Holders

If you already have a mortgage and are making repayments without any issues, the MMR is unlikely to impact your ability to get a mortgage on a new property or remortgage your existing home.

What Should I Do If I Want To Apply For A Mortgage?

While the rules around applying for a mortgage are stricter than they were before, this doesn't mean that you can't get a mortgage, it just means you might have to work harder to evidence your ability to make payments than you would have before 2014. To improve your chances of being approved, before you apply you should:

- 1. Save as big a deposit as you can; the larger your deposit, the lower your interest rate is likely to be. First-time buyers might want to look at Help to Buy ISAs to get more interest on their savings.

- 2. Research the mortgage market, so you understand what type of mortgage you want and how much you want to lend. Speak to your bank to find out what mortgages are available or enlist the services of a mortgage broker.

- 3. Calculate how much you could repay based on current interest rates and after any potential interest rate rises. You can use this to evidence your ability to pay with lenders.

- 4. Reduce your incidentals spending and pay off or reduce the size of any debts; lenders are looking at both sets of outgoings when deciding how large a loan to offer you.

- 5. Know your credit score; if it's lower than you need to get a good interest rate, work on improving it before applying for a mortgage.

- 6. Make sure you are on the electoral roll. Lenders use this to verify your identity.

- 7. Have all your paperwork in order, including bank statement, payslips or P60s, passports and driving licenses and evidence of any income from child benefit, pensions, or self-employment.

- Finally, remember to be realistic. If you are applying for a mortgage, the MMR is designed to make sure you don't over-extend yourself and end up in a position where you can't make repayments. It is much better to apply for a mortgage that you can afford and be approved than ask for one you can't and be turned down.

Deposits

Most banks and building societies used to lend 95% maximum, some more than that. It is now possible, if you look around, to get a high loan to valuation, as there is a lot of competition with low interest rates here to stay for the moment, although as always, lenders will usually require higher deposits. The best source of information for reputable lenders is in the weekend newspapers. However, still, the more that you put down the better deal that you are likely to get from the lender.

Help to Buy equity loan

To be eligible for a Help to Buy: Equity Loan (2021-2023)

- you must be a first-time buyer
- the new build home you buy must fall within the relevant regional price cap.
- You and anyone you're buying a home with must:
- not own a home or residential land now or in the past in the UK or abroad
- not have had any form of sharia mortgage finance.
- Applications made by anyone that is married or in a civil partnership will need a joint application with their spouse or civil partner.
- You must tell us if you or anyone you are buying with has a connection with a homebuilder, as this could affect your eligibility for the equity loan scheme.
- You are not allowed to sublet your home without Homes England's consent.
- To apply for Help to Buy: Equity Loan (2021-2023) you must:
- have a deposit of at least 5% of the purchase price
- reserve a new build home with a registered Help to Buy homebuilder
- arrange a repayment mortgage of at least 25% of the purchase price
- be able to afford the repayments on the equity loan, your repayment mortgage, and other outgoings.

- You can apply from 16 December 2020.

Eligibility Checks

The government will check if you're eligible for the scheme. They will use the eligibility calculator tool to check your monthly income and outgoings, including household bills and estimated mortgage repayments in the calculations. Your repayment mortgage should be less than 4.5 times your gross annual income.

If you have a large deposit and can secure a mortgage without our support, consider if an equity loan is right for you. Getting independent financial advice could help you make the right choice.

Applying for Help to Buy: Equity Loan (2021-2023)

Homebuyers who are eligible for a Help to Buy: Equity Loan can start the application process. More detailed information can be found in the Homebuyers' guide to Help to Buy: Equity Loan (2021-2023)

https://www.gov.uk/government/publications/help-to-buy-equity-loan-buyers-guide

Buying through shared ownership

You can get a shared ownership home through a housing association. You buy a share of your home (between 25% and 75%) and pay rent on the rest. There are different rules in Northern

Ireland and Scotland. Contact your local authority to find out about buying a shared ownership home in Wales.

Eligibility

You can buy a home through shared ownership if your household earns £80,000 a year or less (or £90,000 a year or less in London) and any of the following apply:

- you're a first-time buyer
- you used to own a home, but can't afford to buy one now
- you're an existing shared owner

Older people

If you're aged 55 or over you can buy up to 75% of your home through the Older People's Shared Ownership (OPSO) scheme. Once you own 75% you won't pay rent on the rest.

Disabled people

You can apply for a scheme called home ownership for people with a long-term disability (HOLD) if other Help to Buy scheme properties don't meet your needs, eg you need a ground-floor property. With this scheme you can buy up to 25% of your home. If you're disabled you can also apply for the general shared ownership scheme and own up to 75% of your home.

Buying more shares

You can buy more of your home after you become the owner. This is known as 'staircasing'.The cost of your new share will depend on how much your home is worth when you want to buy the share. It will cost:

- more than your first share if property prices in your area have gone up
- less than your first share if property prices in your area have gone down

The housing association will get your property valued and let you know the cost of your new share. You'll have to pay the valuer's fee.

Selling your home

If you own a share of your home, the housing association has the right to buy it first. This is known as 'first refusal'. The housing association also has the right to find a buyer for your home. If you own 100% of your home, you can sell it yourself.

How to apply

To buy a home through a shared ownership scheme contact the Help to Buy agent in the area where you want to live. For more information go to:

www.helptobuy.gov.uk/equity-loan/find-helptobuy-agent

Joint mortgages

If you want a joint mortgage, as for any other shared loan you and your partner have a shared responsibility for ensuring that the necessary repayments are made. If something happens to one partner then the other has total responsibility for the loan.

Main types of mortgage

Endowment

With this type of mortgage, you have to take out an endowment insurance policy which is then used to pay off the mortgage loan in a lump sum at the end of the term. There are a number of different types designed to achieve the same end:

- Low cost with profits. This is the usual sort of endowment, guaranteeing to pay back part of the loan only. However, because bonuses are likely to be added, it is usually enough to pay off the loan in full;

- Unit linked endowment. With this, the monthly premiums are used to buy units in investment funds. The drawback is that there is no guarantee how much the policy will be worth on maturity, since this depends on how well the investments have performed.

A word of warning. Endowment products were pushed heavily by financial brokers. There was an obsession with them in the 1980's. This is because they earn big commission for those people that sell them. Like a lot of salespeople, motivated by greed salespeople, some advisers failed to reveal the down side.

This is:

-Endowments are investment linked and there is no guarantee that they will have matured sufficiently at the end of the term to repay the mortgage. This leaves you in a mess. A repayment mortgage will definitely have paid off the mortgage at the end of the term. If you change your mortgage and decide that you do not wish to continue with an endowment mortgage, and so cash in the policy early you will almost certainly get a poor return unless it is close to maturity. In the early years of the policy, most of your payments will go towards administration and commission (a fact that your broker does not always reveal). The alternative in these circumstances is to maintain the endowment until it matures, treating it as a stand-alone investment which will, hopefully, make you some money eventually.

Repayment mortgages

This mortgage, where the borrower makes regular repayments to pay the mortgage off over the term is a fairly safe bet. However, if you plan to move house every five years then this will not necessarily be the best mortgage for you. With a repayment mortgage, you pay interest every month but only a small proportion of the capital, particularly in the early years of the mortgage. An endowment mortgage, while more risky, could be better for you under these circumstances, since you can transfer the plan from property to property, while it can, hopefully, grow steadily as it matures.

Pension mortgages

Similar to the other products except that the payments go into a personal pension plan with the remainder after paying the mortgage forming the basis of a pension. The same characteristics apply as to the others.

Interest only mortgage

The borrower pays interest only on the loan, and decides how he or she will pay the loan off at the end. The lender will want to know this too, particularly in the light of the new rules being introduced, mentioned above.

Mixed mortgages

A new development is that one or two lenders now allow borrowers to mix a combination of mortgages in one deal, customising the mortgage to suit each individual.

Foreign currency mortgages

Some foreign banks offer short-term mortgages in the foreign currency of that bank. Their lending criteria can be much more relaxed than trying to borrow from a British lender. The advantage of this sort of mortgage depends on currency fluctuations. If the pound is stable or rises, the borrower benefits. If the pound drops, the borrower will have to pay more. These types of home loans should be left to more sophisticated investors as there is the potential to get into trouble unless you have a clear grasp on the implications of such a mortgage.

Cashbacks

You probably saw the adverts offering large sums of cashback if you took a particular product. If you read the small print, unless you took the highest mortgage available with the highest deposit then you would not get anywhere near such a sum. This mortgage was typical of the many mortgages on offer in the pre-credit crunch times. You would be very hard pushed to see such an offer now.

Buy to Let Mortgages

Buy-to-let (BTL) mortgages are for landlords who buy property to rent it out. The rules around buy-to-let mortgages are similar to those around regular mortgages, but there are some key differences. Read on for more information about how they work, how to get one and what mistakes to avoid.

Who can get a buy-to-let mortgage?

You can get a buy-to-let mortgage if:

- You want to invest in houses or flats.

- You can afford to take a risk. Investing in property is risky, so you shouldn't take out a BTL mortgage if you can't afford to take that risk.

- You already own your own home. You'll struggle to get a buy-to-let mortgage if you don't already own your own home, whether outright or with an outstanding mortgage.

- You have a good credit record and aren't stretched too much on your other borrowings such as your existing mortgage and credit cards.

- You earn £25,000+ a year. Otherwise you might struggle to get a lender to approve your buy-to-let mortgage.

- You're under a certain age. Lenders have upper age limits, typically between 70 or 75. This is the oldest you can be when the mortgage ends not when it starts. For example, if you are 45 when you take out a 25-year mortgage it will finish when you're 70.

How do buy-to-let mortgages work?

Buy-to-let mortgages are a lot like ordinary mortgages, but with some key differences:

- Interest rates on buy-to-let mortgages are usually higher.
- The fees also tend to be much higher.

- The minimum deposit for a buy-to-let mortgage is usually 25% of the property's value (although it can vary between 20-40%).

- Most BTL mortgages are interest-only. This means you don't pay anything each month, but at the end of the mortgage term you repay the capital in full.

- Most BTL mortgage lending is not regulated by the Financial Conduct Authority (FCA). There are exceptions, for example, if you wish to let the property to a close family member (e.g. spouse, civil partner, child, grandparent, parent or sibling). These are often referred to as a consumer buy to let mortgages and are assessed according to the same strict affordability rules as a residential mortgage.

How much you can you borrow for buy-to-let mortgages

The maximum you can borrow is linked to the amount of rental income you expect to receive. Lenders typically need the rental income to be a 25–30% higher than your mortgage payment. To find out what your rent might be talk to local letting agents, or check the local press and online to find out how much similar properties are rented for.

Where to get a buy-to-let mortgage

Most of the big banks and some specialist lenders offer BTL mortgages. It's a good idea to talk to a mortgage broker before you take out a buy-to-let mortgage, as they will help you choose the most suitable deal for you.

Using price comparison websites

Comparison websites are a good starting point for anyone trying to find a mortgage tailored to their needs. the following are the most popular.

- Moneyfacts
- Money Saving Expert
- MoneySuperMarket
- Which?

Comparison websites won't all give you the same results, so make sure you use more than one site before making a decision. It is also important to do some research into the type of product and features you need before making a purchase or changing supplier.

Plan for times when there's no rent coming in

Don't assume that your property will always have tenants. There will almost certainly be 'voids' when the property is unoccupied or rent isn't paid and you'll need to have a financial 'cushion' to meet your mortgage payments. When you do have rent coming in, use some of it to top up your savings account. You might also need savings for major repair bills. For example, the boiler might break down, or there may be a blocked drain.

Stamp Duty Land Tax (SDLT)for buy to let properties is an extra 3% on top of the current SDLT rate bands.

What to do if you feel that you have been given wrong advice

The mortgage lending market is very complicated and many people have suffered at the hands of financial advisors and others who have given incorrect advice. Mortgage regulation has not been very tight. However, the basic framework is as follows:

- Sales of mortgage linked investments like endowments or pensions are regulated by the Financial Conduct Authority. Anyone selling investments must be qualified and registered and must be able to clearly demonstrate that the policy that they have recommended is suitable. All registered individuals and firms are inspected by regulators and can be fined or expelled from the industry if guilty of wrongly selling products. By contrast, information on mortgages is currently regulated by the industry only, voluntarily, under a code of mortgage practice sponsored by the Council of Mortgage Lenders. Although most of the big players are signed up to the code there are still some who are not. Check first before taking advice.

How to complain

- Complain first to the company that sold you the product, going through its internal complaints procedure.
- If you are unhappy with the firm's decision, approach the

relevant complaints body. For mortgage advisors employed directly by lenders, or complaints about lenders generally, contact the Financial Ombudsman Service on 0800 023 4 567 or www.financial-ombudsman.org.uk

- For mortgage lenders which are not building societies or banks but which are signed up to the mortgage code, the Chartered Institute of Arbitrators 020 7421 7455 www.ciarb.org will assist.

- If your complaint is about a mortgage broker, contact the Chartered Institute of Arbitrators which may be able to help if the firm is registered under the code.

- Complaints about endowments, pensions and other investments is handled by the Financial Conduct Authority 0800 111 67 68 www.fca..org.uk and are dealt with by the financial ombudsman Service. The most common complaint is to do with endowments. A lot of people bought products they came to regret. They are a major source of profit to the provider-and all those in between-but the person left holding the problem is the consumer. If you believe that you have been given bad advice about anything to do with the insurance or investment side of a product then you should approach the Financial Services Authority. The Building Society Association or the British Bankers Association have free publications that should help you. In addition, the Consumers Association, "Which" runs regular articles on mortgages. Remember - always ask questions. Never rush into anything. Always take advice if you are uncertain.

Banks and building societies themselves are usually a better source, a safer source than individual advisers.

Borrowing and the internet

Almost all lenders have their own sites and many operate internet only loans with keener rates than those available on the high street. But there are also growing numbers of mortgage broker sites, offering mortgage calculators so that you can work out how much you can afford to borrow and how much the true cost of your loan will be. A list of internet sites can be found in the useful addresses and websites section at the back of this book.

****

Chapter 5

Selling Your Home

Estate agents

Ask for quotes from at least three agents before instructing one or more of them. The fee is normally based on the selling price of the house and is between 1 - 3 per cent of the final selling price. However, VAT (currently 20%) will be added on to this. The next chapter on conveyancing gives an idea of the processes involved once a buyer is found.

DIY Selling

If you want to save the cost of instructing an agent to sell your house, you could try to sell it yourself. Around 4 - 5% of homes in the UK are sold privately. There are a number of useful guides which are dedicated to this subject. One site worth visiting is www.yopa.co.uk/homeowners-hub/guide-selling-house-privately.

Setting the price if selling yourself

You need to see how much similar properties are sold for in the area. There are numerous firms on the web who will provide you with a valuation. If this proves difficult, get a professional valuation.

Contact the Royal Institution of Chartered Surveyors who will advise you. A valuation report will only value and will not assess structural soundness. A survey is needed for that. Put together the sales particulars in the same way that an estate agent would. It is advisable to put a disclaimer on these details such as "these particulars are believed to be accurate and are set out as a general outline only for the guidance of interested buyers. They do not constitute, nor constitute parts of, an offer or contract.

Advertising your property independently

There are a number of ways you can advertise your property. Local papers will advertise for you and also there are free ad papers. In addition, there are a number of companies with a computerised sales network who will charge you a flat fee for advertising. Be accurate with the details - you may leave yourself open to damages through misrepresentation. If an offer is made to you then you should then hand matters over to your solicitor. As discussed, some sellers handle their own conveyancing lock stock and barrel. This includes the legal side. However, this book cannot advise you on legal conveyancing. That is a separate matter. Suffice to say that it follows a standard format. It is easier, in the light of the reduced prices available to appoint a solicitor to do this side for you.

Selling using online agents

Online estate agents can help you sell your property without using a traditional high-street agent. Run via websites and call centres, they tend to offer a more basic service than you'd receive from a high-street agent and, as a result, they charge lower fees. Two types of online agents have emerged over the last few years. Online-only estate agents require the seller to do most of the work themselves, from taking photos and creating an advert to handling buyer enquiries, conducting viewings and negotiating offers. But many online-only estate agents have now evolved into hybrid agencies, employing 'local property experts' to handle buyer enquiries, accompany viewings and negotiate offers.

How do online estate agents work?
The services offered by online estate agents - particularly hybrid agencies - are similar to those offered by high-street agents, but often in a more stripped-back form. Most online estate agents now offer the option of valuing and marketing your home and arranging property viewings. Many can also negotiate and accept offers on your behalf, and liaise with your conveyancer, other estate agents and buyers until the sale is complete. These services usually incur a higher fee than the basic service.

While high-street estate agents will usually charge you a percentage of your property's selling price, online estate agents generally charge fixed fees. This means that using an online agent is often much cheaper, especially if your home is worth a lot of money. For example, if you sold a property worth £250,000 using a high-street estate agency that charged 1.3% commission, you'd pay £3,250. Online estate agents typically charge a flat fee of between £300 and £1,500, regardless of the value of your property.

A major downside of online estate agents' lower prices is that you'll often have to pay up front, regardless of whether they end up selling your home or not. Paying a fixed fee also reduces the agent's incentive to sell your property for the highest possible price. However, some online estate agents offer the option to pay once you've completed the sale but for a slightly higher price, reducing the risk of wasting your money. Some also offer a deferred payment option, where you pay at a defined point in the future, for example, 10 or 12 months down the line. This may involve entering into a credit agreement with the agency, so make sure you fully understand the terms before signing on the dotted line.

Property valuations

An online-only agent is likely to use online data to value your home, while hybrid online estate agents will send a 'local expert' to provide a valuation. However, you won't necessarily get a valuer with specific knowledge of the local market.

Remember you don't have to use the valuation provided. Ask three firms – high street or online – and go with an average, or whatever you think is the right price based on recent similar examples you've found through your own research. Inviting a variety of companies to value your home and talking to them about their sales process will also enable you to more deeply understand the differences between online and high street agents.

Marketeting

Online estate agents will list your home on their site as well as other online property portals such as Rightmove and Zoopla. Some will install a 'for sale' sign outside your house, although they might charge extra for this. High street estate agents will do all of the above as a standard part of their service, and can also place adverts in their branch windows.

Viewings

The default option with most online estate agents is that you conduct the viewings yourself. However, a lot of online agents now offer accompanied viewings for an extra fee of around £300, or as part of a more expensive package than their standard offering.

Buyer vetting

Some (though not all) online estate agents will vet buyers, typically getting details of names, finances and whether potential buyers are already part of a chain.

Communicate with an online agent

Someone will visit to take photographs and create floor plans if you sign up for this option, and you'll meet the 'local property expert' if the agency sends one round. However, all other contact will usually be via email or phone - and many online estate agencies offer online portals where you can access helplines or chat services outside traditional working hours, with some offering 24/7 support.

Rights when using an online estate agent

Online estate agents are governed by the same regulations that cover high street estate agents.as with high street agents, online estate agents must be members of a government-approved redress scheme – the Property Ombudsman Limited or the Property Redress Scheme. Your agent has to be clear about which redress scheme they are a member of, and the scheme should be your first port of call if you have a problem.Trading Standards will also investigate agents that it believes have acted in breach of the 1979 Estate Agent Act, which sets out minimum standards of conduct for estate agents.

Pros and cons of online estate agents

Online estate agents can be a great money-saving option when you're selling your house, but you should be aware of the pros and cons of these services before making a decision.

Pros of using an online estate agent:

- Fees: in most cases, using an online estate agent will be a lot cheaper than using a high-street agent. The more expensive your home is, the more you stand to save if they charge a flat fee.

- Convenience: it can sometimes be easier to get hold of online estate agents. Their call centres are open during evenings and weekends, so they are able to deal with queries outside of working hours (although some high-street agents offer this, too).
- Flexibility: packages can be tailored to your specific requirements, and you can often track viewings and feedback online (some high-street agents also offer this).
- Freedom to use multiple agents: generally, there is no contract period, which means you can instruct other estate agents if you wish.

Cons of using an online estate agent

- Lack of local knowledge: even online agents with regional reps could struggle to compete with a high-street agent who knows your neighbourhood and its property market inside out.
- Legwork: some online estate agents won't negotiate offers or act as a middleman to progress your sale to completion. Having to manage communications with buyers and solicitors on your own can be time-consuming and stressful.
- Viewings: you usually have to conduct viewings yourself, so you'll need to be comfortable showing strangers around your

home and be available during evenings and weekends.

- Paying up front: if you opt for this type of package, you won't be paying on results. In fact, you'll have to pay even if that company doesn't end up selling your house.

- Selling price: because most online estate agents charge a flat fee rather than commission, they have less incentive to get the best price for you. That said, they have reputations to maintain, and many companies claim they usually achieve the asking price.

Selling at Auction

Advantages of auction

In chapter 3, we looked at buying properties at auction. Here are a few tips for you when selling a property at auction. An auction is an efficient and cost effective way of selling property and if prepared properly with intensive marketing, advertising and mailing, will result in the greatest possible exposure of the lots offered. To maximize the effectiveness of the marketing, considerable thought must be given to the guide price, which needs to be tailored to generate competitive bidding in the auction room, thus ensuring that the best price is being achieved. Although some properties are more suitable for sale by private treaty, taking this route does present uncertainties over terms such as sale price and timing of exchange and completion.

Selling by auction however, offers a high degree of certainty that a sale will be achieved on a given day and, significantly, on the fall of the gavel an immediate binding contract is formed. As no further negotiation is permitted the entire sale process, from instruction to exchange of contracts can be, is achieved within as little as six to eight weeks. For vendors with a large number of properties to sell, auctions provide a highly efficient method of sale allowing for a total or phased disposal programme selling in individual lots thus maximising receipts. For those selling in a fiduciary capacity, there is the added advantage of the sale being entirely open and transparent. Most types of property are suitable for auction provided that a realistic reserve price is agreed.

Quick Results

The entire process, from instruction to exchange of contracts, can be achieved within as little as six to eight weeks.

****

Chapter 6

Conveyancing a Property

We have talked briefly about conveyancing in an earlier chapter. Conveyancing, or the practice of conveyancing, is about how to transfer the ownership of land and property from one person or organisation to another. Land and property can include freehold property, leasehold property (residential) or can include business leases. *Essentially, the process of conveyancing lays down clear procedures for the conveyancer and also sets out each party's position during the sale or acquisition.*

Most conveyancing, in particular relatively simple residential transactions, is carried out electronically, with the Land Registry aiming to move towards a complete digital process in the next few years. Before understanding the process of conveyancing, however, it is essential to understand something about the legal forms of ownership of property.

Legal ownership of property

There are two main forms of legal ownership of property in Great Britain. If you are about to embark on the sale or acquisition of a house or flat (or business) then you will be dealing in the main with either freehold or leasehold property. It is very rare indeed to find other forms of ownership, although the government has introduced a form of ownership called 'common hold' that in essence creates the freehold ownership of flats, with common responsibility for communal areas.

Freehold property

In general, if you own the freehold of a house or a piece of land, then you will be the outright owner with no fixed period of time and no one else to answer to (with the exception of statutory authorities). There may be registered restrictions on title, which will be discussed later. The property will probably be subject to a mortgage so the only other overriding interest will be that of the bank or the building society. The responsibility for repairs and maintenance and general upkeep will be the freeholders. The law can intervene if certain standards are not maintained. The deed to your house will be known as the "freehold transfer document" which will contain any rights and obligations. Usually, the transfer document will list any "encumbrances" (restrictions) on the use of the land, such as rights of way of other parties, sales restrictions etc. The deeds to your home are the most important documentation.

As we will see later, without deeds and historical data, such as the root of title, it can be rather complicated selling property. This is why the system of land registration in use in this country has greatly simplified property transactions. *Any person owning freehold property is free to create another interest in land, such as a lease or a weekly or monthly tenancy, subject to any restrictions the transfer may contain.*

Leasehold property

If a person lives in a property owned by someone else and has an agreement for a period of time, usually a long period, over 21 years and up to 99 years or 125 years, in some cases 999 years, then they are a leaseholder.

The conveyancing of leasehold property is, potentially, far more problematic than freehold property, particularly when the flat is in a block with a number of units. The lease is a contract between landlord and tenant which lays down the rights and obligations of both parties and should be read thoroughly by both the leaseholder and, in particular, the conveyancer. Once signed then the purchaser is bound by all the clauses in the contract. It is worth taking a little time looking at the nature of a lease before discussing the rather more complex process of conveyancing. Again, it has to be stated that it is of the utmost importance that both the purchaser and the vendor understand the nature of a lease.

The lease-Preamble

The start of a lease is called the preamble. This defines the landlord and purchaser and also the nature of the property in question (the demise). It will also detail the remaining period of the lease.

Leaseholders covenants

Covenants are best understood as obligations and responsibilities. Leaseholder's covenants are therefore a list of things that leaseholders should do, such as pay their service charges and keep the interior of the dwelling in good repair and not to, for example, alter the structure. The landlord's covenants will set out the obligations of the landlord, which is usually to maintain the structure and exterior of the block, light common parts etc.

One unifying theme of all leasehold property is that, notwithstanding the landlord's responsibilities, it is the leaseholder who will pay for everything out of a service charge.

Leases will make detailed provisions for the setting, managing and charging of service charges, which should include a section on accounting. All landlords of leaseholders are accountable under the Landlord and Tenant Act 1985, as amended. These Acts will regulate the way a landlord treats a leaseholder in the charging and accounting of service charges.

In addition, the 1996 Housing Act, as amended by the 2002 Commonhold and Leasehold Reform Act has provided further legislation protecting leaseholders by introducing the right of leaseholders to go to Firs Tier Tribunals if they are unhappy with levels and management of charges and also to carry out audits of charges. It is vital that, when buying a leasehold property that you read the lease. Leases tend to be different from each other and nothing can be assumed. When you buy a property, ensure that the person selling has paid all debts and has contributed to some form of "sinking fund" whereby provision has been built up for major repairs in the future. Make sure that you will not be landed with big bills after moving in and that, if you are, there is money to deal with them. After a lease has been signed then there is little or no recourse to recoup any money owed.

These are all the finer points of leases and the conveyancer has to be very vigilant. In particular read the schedules to the lease as these sometimes contain rather more detail. One of the main differences between leasehold and freehold property is that the lease is a long tenancy agreement which contains provisions which give the landlord rather a lot of power to manage (or mismanage) and it is always a (remote) possibility that a leaseholder can be forced to give up his or her home in the event of non-compliance with the terms of the lease. This is known as forfeiture.

Under legislation referred to earlier, a new 'no fault right to manage' has been introduced. This enables leaseholders who are unhappy with the management of their property, to take over the management with relative ease. The Act applies to most landlords, with the exception of Local Authorities. These powers go a long way to curb the excesses or inefficiencies of numerous landlords and provide more control and greater security for leaseholders.

Check points

There are key areas of a lease that should be checked when purchasing. Some have already been discussed.

- What is the term left on the lease?
- Is the preamble clear, i.e. is the area which details landlord, tenant and demised (sold) premises, clear?
- Is the lease assignable- i.e. can you pass on the lease without landlords permission or does it need surrendering at sale or a license to assign?
- What is the ground rent and how frequently will you pay it?
- What is the level of service charge, if any, and how is it collected, apportioned, managed and accounted for?
- What are the general restrictions in the lease, can you have pets for example, can you park cars and do you have a designated space?
- What are the respective repairing obligations? As we have seen, the leaseholder will pay anyway but the landlord and leaseholder will hold respective responsibilities. This is an important point because occasionally, there is no stated responsibility for upkeep and the environment deteriorates as a consequence, diminishing the value of the property.

Two systems of conveyancing

After gaining an understanding of the nature of the interest in land that you are buying, it is absolutely essential to understand the two systems of conveyancing property in existence, as this will determine, not so much the procedure because the initial basic steps in conveyancing, such as carrying out searches, are common to both forms of land, registered and unregistered, but the way you go about the process and the final registration are different.

Registered and unregistered land

In England and Wales the method of conveyancing to be used in each particular transaction very much depends on whether the land is *registered* or *unregistered* land. If the title, or proof of ownership, of land and property has been registered under the Land Registration Acts 1925-86 then the Land Registry (see below) will be able to furnish the would-be conveyancer with such documentation as is required to establish ownership, third party rights etc. If the land has not been registered then proof of ownership of the land in question must be traced through the title deeds.

Registered land

As more and more conveyancing is falling within the remit of the Land Registry, because it is compulsory to register land throughout England and Wales, it is worth outlining this system briefly at this stage. The Land Registration Acts of 1925 established the Land Registry (HM Land Registry). The Land Registry is a department of the Civil Service, at its head is the Chief Land Registrar. All applications to the Land Registry must be made within the district in question. There is a specific terminology in use within conveyancing, particularly within the land registry:

- *a piece of land*, or parcel of land is known as a *registered title*
- the owner of land is referred to as the *registered proprietor*
- a conveyance of registered land is called *a transfer*
- a transaction involving registered land is known as *a dealing*

The main difference between the two types of conveyancing *registered* and *unregistered* concerns what is known *as proof of title*. In the case of land that is unregistered the owner will prove title by showing the would-be purchaser the documentary evidence which shows how he or she came to own the land and property.

In the case of registered land the owner has to show simply that he or she is registered at the Land Registry as the registered proprietor. Proof of registration is proof of ownership, which is unequivocal. In registered land the documents proving ownership are replaced by the fact of registration. Each separate title or ownership of land has a title number, which the Land Registry uses to trace ownership, or confirm ownership. The description of each title on the register is identified by the *title number,* described by reference to the filed plan (indicating limits and extent of ownership). With registered conveyancing the Land Registry keeps the register of title and file plan and title. The owner (proprietor) is issued with a Land Certificate. If the land in question is subject to a mortgage then the mortgagee is issued with a Land Certificate.

Production of the Land Certificate

With registered land, whenever there is a sale, or disposition, then the Land Certificate must be produced to the Land Registry in the appropriate district. If proved that a Certificate is lost or destroyed then a new one can be issued by the Land Registry.

The key steps in the process of conveyancing property

Before the buyer exchanges contracts on a property, whether registered or unregistered, and then completes the purchase a number of searches are always carried out. These are:

Enquiry's before contract
Local land charges search
Enquiry's of the local authority
Index map search

Making enquiry's before contract

These are enquiry's to the seller, or the Vendor of the property and are aimed at revealing certain facts about the property that the seller has no legal obligation to disclose to the buyer. There are certain matters, which are always raised. These are:

- Whether there are any existing boundary disputes
- What services are supplied to the property, whether electricity, gas or other
- Any easements or covenants in the lease. These are stipulations

in the lease, which give other certain rights, such as rights of way.

- Any guarantees in existence

- *Planning considerations*
- Adverse rights affecting the property
- Any fixtures and fittings
- Whether there has been any breach of restriction affecting the property

If the property is newly built, information will be required concerning any outstanding works or future guarantees of remedying defects. Where a property is leasehold, information will be required about the lessor.

Registered conveyancers will use a standard form to raise these enquiries, so that the initial search is exhaustive. As part of the move towards openness in the process of buying and selling property, and also an attempt to speed up the process of sale, the Law Society has introduced new forms which the solicitor, or buyer if carrying out his or her own conveyancing, is being encouraged to use. These are Seller's Property Information Forms relating to freehold and leasehold property, that the seller and solicitor will respectively fill in, a form relating to fixtures, fittings and contents and a form relating to complete information and requisitions on title. These forms can be obtained from a legal stationers, and have the pre-fix Prop 1-7. If a conveyancer is being used then it is advisable to ask whether or not they are using these newly introduced forms. The main point is that you should think long and hard about the type of questions that should be raised. The vendor does not have to answer the questions, but beware a vendor who refuses to disclose answers. Answers given by the vendor do not form part of the subsequent contract and therefore cannot be used against that person in the event of future problems. However, the Misrepresentations Act of 1976 could be evoked if a deliberate misrepresentation has caused problems.

Local land charges search

The Local Land Charges Act 1975 requires District Councils, London Borough Councils and the City of London Corporation to maintain a Local Land Charges Registry for the area.

Local land charges can be divided into two areas:

- Financial charges on the land for work carried out by the local authority
- restrictions on the use of land

- The register is further divided into twelve parts:
- general financial charges
- specific financial charges

- planning charges
- miscellaneous charges and provisions
- charges for improvements of ways over fenland
- land compensation charges
- new town charges
- civil aviation charges
- open cast coal mining charges
- listed buildings charges
- light obstruction notices
- drainage scheme charges

All charges are enforceable by the local authority except g and i, which are enforced by statutory bodies and private individuals generally. A buyer should search in all parts of this particular register and this can be done by a personal or official search. A personal search, as the name suggests, involves the individual or their agent attending at the local authority office and, on paying the relevant fee, personally searching the register. The charges are registered against the land concerned and not against the owner. The official search is the one most favoured because, in the event of missing a vital piece of information the chances of compensation are far higher than with a personal search.

With the official search a requisition for a search and for an official certificate of search is sent to the Registrar of Local Land Charges for the area within which the land is situated. There is a fee and the search is carried out by the Registrars staff, which results in a certificate being sent to the person making the request, which clearly outlines any charges. The Registrar may require a plan of the land as well as the postal address. Separate searches are made of each parcel of land being purchased.

Local authority searches

There is a standard form in use for these particular types of searches. This is known as "Con 29 England and Wales" Revised July 2016, with the format of the form differing slightly for inner London boroughs. Any of the forms in the process can be obtained from legal stationers.

The standard forms in use contain a statement to the effect that the local authority is not responsible for errors unless negligence is proved. Many of the enquiries relate specifically to planning matters, whilst other elements of the search are concerned about roads and whether they are adopted and whether there are likely to be any costs falling onto property owners.

We will be considering planning matters concerning the individual property a little later. Other enquiry's relate to possible construction of new roads which may affect the property, the location of sewers and pipes and whether the property is in an area of compulsory registration of title, a smoke control area or slum clearance area. The form used is so constructed that part 2 of the form contains questions, which must be initialled by the purchaser before they are answered. Again these questions cover planning and other matters. Other enquiry's can be asked by the individual, which are answered at the authorities discretion. In addition to the above, which are the major searches, there are others that the conveyancer has to be aware of. These are as follows:

Searches in the Index map and parcels index of the Land register

If the land has been registered the title will be disclosed and whether it is registered leasehold or freehold. Registered rent charges are also disclosed by the search. (See chapter 7.)

Commons Registration Act (1965) search

This act imposes a duty on County Councils to keep a register relating to village greens and common land and interests over them, such as right of way.

Coal mining search

The request for this search if relevant, is designed to reveal the whereabouts of mineshafts and should be sent to the local Area Coal Board office, or its equivalent. The search will disclose past workings and any subsidence, proposed future workings and the proximity of opencast workings.

It is usually well known if there is a problem, or potential problem with coal mining in an area and this search is essential if that is the case.

Other enquiry's

There are a number of other bodies from which it might be appropriate to request a search. These include British Rail, statutory undertakers such as electricity and gas boards, planning authorities generally, rent assessment committees and so on. These will only usually be necessary if there is a direct link between the property being purchased and a particular circumstance within an area or property.

Planning matters relating to specific properties

It is obviously very necessary to determine whether or not any illegal alterations have been carried out to the property you wish to purchase, before reaching the point of exchange of contracts. This is to ensure that the vendor has complied with relevant planning legislation, if any material changes have been made, and that you will not be required at a later date to carry out remedial work. The Local Authority maintains a register of planning applications relating to properties within their boundaries. In addition, the register will also reveal any planning enforcement notices in force against a particular property.

Questions such as these, and also any questions relating to the effect of Structure or Local plans, (specific plans relating to local and borough wide plans for the future) should be made in writing to the local authority or an individual search can be carried out. Usually they are carried out if there is any suspicion that planning regulations may have been breached. In addition, there may be other considerations, such as whether the building is listed or whether tree preservation orders relating to trees within the cartilage of the property are in force. It is certainly essential to know about these. It is highly recommended that all of these searches are carried out and completed before contracts are exchanged.

The contract for sale

As with many other transactions, a sale of land is effected through a contract. However, a contract, which deals with the sale of land, is governed by the requirements of the Law of Property (miscellaneous provisions) Act 1989, the equitable doctrine of specific performance and the duty of the vendor to provide title to the property.

The Law of Property Act (Miscellaneous provisions) 1988 provides that contracts dealing with the sale of land after 26th September 1989 must be in writing. The contract must contain all the terms and agreements to which the respective parties to the transaction have agreed. The provisions of the Act do not apply to sales at a public auction, contracts to grant a short lease and contracts regulated under the Financial Services Act 1986. If the person purchasing is doing so through an agent then the agent must have authority to act on behalf of the purchaser. Examples of agents are auctioneers and solicitors, also estate agents. If the phrase "subject to contract" is used in a sale then the intention of both parties to the contract is that neither are contractually bound until a formal contract has been agreed by the parties, signed and exchanged.

Therefore, the words "subject to contract" are a protective device, although it is not good to depend on the use of these words throughout a transaction

Procedures in the formation of contract

The vendor's solicitor will usually draw up an initial contract of sale. This is because only this person has access to all the necessary initial documents to begin to effect a contract. The draft contract is prepared in two parts and sent to the purchaser's solicitor (if using a solicitor), the other side will approve or amend the contract as necessary. Both sides must agree to any proposed amendments. After agreement has been reached, the vendor's solicitor will retain one copy of the contract and send the other copy to the solicitor or person acting for the other side. The next stage is for the vendors solicitor to engross (sign and formalise) the contract in two parts. Both parts are then sent to the purchaser's solicitor or other agent who checks that they are correct then sends one part back to the vendor's solicitor.

The Contents of a contract

A contract will be in two parts, *the particulars of sale* and the *conditions of sale*. The particulars of sale give a physical description of the land and also of the interest, which is being sold. A property must be described accurately and a plan may be attached to the contract to emphasize or illustrate what is in the contract. The particulars will also outline whether the property is freehold or leasehold and what kind of lease the vendor is assigning, i.e., head lease (where vendor is owner of the freehold) or underlease, where the vendor is not.

It is very important to determine what kind of lease it is that is being assigned, indeed whether it is assignable or whether permission is needed from the landlord and it is recommended that a solicitor handle this transaction. This is because any purchaser of a lease can find his or her interest jeopardized by the nature of the lease. Where a sub-lease, or under lease is being purchased, the purchasers interest can be forfeited by the actions of the head lessee, the actions of this person being out of control of the purchaser.

Rights, such as easements and also restrictive covenants, which are for the benefit of the land, should be expressly referred to in the particulars of sale. In addition, the vendor should refer to any latent defects affecting his or her property, if known. This includes any encumbrances, which may affect the property.

Misdescription

If the property in the particulars of sale is described wrongly, i.e. there is a mis-statement of fact, such as describing leasehold as freehold land, calling an under-lease a lease or leaving out something that misleads the buyer, in other words, if the misdescription is material, then the purchaser is entitled to rescind the contract. Essentially the contract must describe what is being sold and if it does not, and the buyer is mislead then the contract is inaccurate. If the misdescription is immaterial and insubstantial, and there has been no misrepresentation then the purchaser cannot rescind the contract. However, if the misdescription has affected the purchase price of the property then the purchaser can insist on a reduction in the asking price. The purchaser should claim this compensation before completion takes place. The vendor has no right to rescind the contract if the misdescription is in the purchaser's favour, for example, the area of land sold is greater than that intended. Neither can the vendor compel the purchaser to pay an increased purchase price

Misrepresentation

Misrepresentation is an untrue statement of fact made by one party or his or her agent, which induces the other party to enter into the contract. An opinion and a statement of intention must be distinguished from a statement of fact.

There are three types of misrepresentation, fraudulent misrepresentation, negligent misrepresentation and innocent misrepresentation.

Fraudulent misrepresentation is a false statement made knowingly or without belief in its truth, or recklessly. The innocent party may sue through the tort of negligence either before or after the contract is complete and rescind the contract. Negligent misrepresentation, although not fraudulent, is where the vendor or his or her agents cannot prove that the statement they made in relation to the contract was correct.

Remedies available are damages or rescission of the contract. Innocent misrepresentation is where the statement made was neither fraudulently or negligently but is still an untrue statement. Rescission is available for this particular type of misrepresentation. Rescission of contract generally is available under the Misrepresentation Act 1967 s 2(2).

Non-disclosure

Generally, in the law of contract, there is the principle of "caveat emptor" "let the buyer beware". In other words, it is up to the purchaser to ensure that what he or she is buying is worth the money paid for it. Earlier we talked about the importance of searches and also, particularly, the importance of the structural survey. Although the vendor has some responsibility to reveal any defects in the property it is always very advisable for the purchaser to ensure that all checks prior to purchase are carried out thoroughly.

Signing the contract

The vendors solicitor will obtain the vendors signature to the contract, when he is satisfied that the vendor can sell what he is purporting to do through the contract. The purchaser's solicitor or agent will do the same, having checked the replies to all enquiry's before contract. It is also essential to check that a mortgage offer has been made and accepted.

Exchanging contracts

Neither party to the sale is legally bound until there has been an exchange of contracts. At one time, a face-to-face exchange would have taken place. However, with the rapid increases in property transactions this rarely happens nowadays. Exchange by post or telephone is more common.

The purchaser will post his or her part of the contract together with the appropriate cheque, or bank transfer, to cover the agreed deposit to the purchaser's solicitor or person acting on behalf of that person. The deposit is usually 10% of the purchase price although there are variations on this theme. The amounts are agreed between buyer and seller. The purchaser's solicitor will usually insert the agreed completion date. On receiving this part of the contract the vendor will add his or her part and send this off in exchange. At this stage, both parties become bound under the contract.

Completion

The requirements concerning completion are detailed thoroughly in the general conditions of sale. Payment on completion is one such detail. Payment on completion should be by one of the following methods:

- legal tender;
- bankers draft;
- an unconditional authority to release any deposit by the stakeholder
- any other method agreed with the vendor.

At common law, completion takes place whenever the vendor wishes and payment is to be made by legal tender. Also dealt with in the general conditions is failure to complete and notices to complete. Failure to complete can cause difficulty for one of the other parties and the aggrieved party can serve notice on the other to complete by a specific date. The notice has the effect of making "time of the essence" which means that a specific date is attached to completion, after which the contract is discharged. It is worth mentioning here that it is very advisable indeed to be aware of scams that have been taking place which have cost purchasers dear. This is a sophisticated email scam. Fraudsters are intercepting emails between homebuyers, sellers and their solicitors to target the large sums of money that are exchanged in property transactions. The criminals hijack or spoof the client or solicitors email accounts and provide a bank account into which they instruct funds to be sent. they then drain the money as soon as possible. It can then be very difficult for the purchaser to get the money back.

In the light of this, if you are involved in selling or buying a property, at the point of making any transaction, you should contact the actual firm itself, if necessary going down to see them, to check that all bank account details are correct.

It is always advisable to instruct a solicitor in your home town so that you can readily go to see them if necessary.

Return of pre-contract deposits

The vendor must return any deposit paid to the purchaser if the purchaser drops out before the exchange of contracts. This cannot be prevented and was the subject of a House of Lords ruling.

The position of the parties after exchange of contracts

Once a contract has been exchanged, the purchaser is the beneficial owner of the property, with the vendor owning the property on trust for the purchaser. The vendor is entitled to any rents or other profits from the land during this period, has the right to retain the property until final payments have been made and has a lien (charge/right) over the property in respect of any unpaid purchase monies. The vendor is bound to take reasonable care of the property and should not let the property fall into disrepair or other damages to be caused during the period between exchange and completion. If completion does not take place at the allotted time and the fault is the purchasers then interest can be charged on the money due.

The purchaser, as beneficial owner of the property is entitled to any increase in the value of the land and buildings but not profits arising. The purchaser has a right of lien over the property, the same as the vendor, in respect of any part of the purchase price paid prior to completion.

Bankruptcy of the vendor

In the unfortunate event of the vendor going bankrupt in between exchange and completion, the normal principles of bankruptcy apply so that the trustee in bankruptcy steps in to the vendor's shoes. The purchaser can be compelled to complete the sale. The trustee in bankruptcy is obliged to complete the sale if the purchaser tenders the purchase money on the completion day.

Bankruptcy of the purchaser

When a purchaser is declared bankrupt in between sale and completion all of his or her property vests in the trustee in bankruptcy. In these circumstances, the vendor can keep any deposit due to him.

Death of Vendor or purchaser

The personal representatives of a deceased vendor can compel the purchaser to sell. The money is conveyed to those representatives who will hold the money in accordance with the terms of any will or in accordance with the rules relating to intestacy if there is no will.

The same position applies to the purchaser's representatives, who can be compelled by the vendor to complete the purchase and who can hold money on the purchaser's behalf.

****

Chapter 7

Planning Moving Arrangements

_____

At this stage, you will either have sold your home and /or be ready to move into a new one. The process of moving home is closely linked with the completion of the purchase of another home. That is, assuming that you are moving to another bought property. Of course, you may be moving to a rented home. However you choose to time your move, there are certain core tasks, as follows:

- Finalise removal and storage arrangements
- Contact electricity/gas/phone/cable companies and any other relevant company to tell them your moving date
- Organise your funds so that you can transfer all remaining money needed to complete the sale into your solicitors account for him/her to pay the sellers solicitor

One main question is: do you get a removal firm or do you do it yourself?

DIY moves

This is cheaper than hiring a removal company, especially if you have a few possessions or no big items of furniture. You will also need willing and able friends. However, do not take the decision to move yourself lightly. Think carefully about the amount of furniture that you have and the fact that your house may be a particularly difficult site to move from.

Using professionals

Professionals know what they are doing and can leave you to organise all the other aspects of moving whilst they do the donkey work. This may cost you more money. However, it may be well worth it. Use a firm which is a member of the British Association of Removers (www.bar.co.uk). Members of this body have to adhere to a code of professional practice, meet minimum standards and provide emergency service and finance guarantees.

Removers can offer various levels of packing services. The most expensive option is for the remover to pack everything. The second most expensive option is for them to pack the breakable things such as glass. The cheapest way is for the removers to provide crates and for you to do your own packing.

If you are going for the professional option:

- Get two or three estimates. You can find the names of local firms through the British Association of Removers or through the local press. There are a growing number of websites that include quotes from removal firms (see below for one of the main ones)

- You should expect estimators to go through your whole property including gardens and loft
- Check whether your possessions will be covered by your household insurance policy and extend the cover if they are not.
- Don't wait to exchange contracts to organise removers.

The following Website may be useful:
www.reallymoving.com

This site was launched in 1999 and is the leading provider of online removal services. Registering on the site will get you three quotes from removers. It also covers solicitors, surveyors and others involved in the buying and selling process.

Contacting utilities

A boring but essential task is to contact all of the companies that provide you with services to tell them that you have moved. This should be done after you exchange contracts, obtaining meter readings etc. Most utilities will ask you for confirmation of your new address and moving date in writing. If you cannot face this task then use the following website:

www.iammoving.com

This site was started in 1999 by a consortium of investors and industry figures. The claim is to be the UK's first free online change of address service. You register, enter your old and new address, supply account numbers and meter readings where relevant and iammoving will send the information to the appropriate companies. The process is quick and relatively uncomplicated.

****

Chapter 8

Buying and Selling in Scotland

Scotland has it own system of law, and buying and selling a house or flat is quite a different process from doing so in England, Wales or Northern Ireland. The system generally works more quickly and there is less risk of gazumping.

Looking for property

Solicitors, property centres and offices. These are the largest source of properties available in Scotland. Often found in town centres, the property centres provide information in a similar way to estate agents outside Scotland. Of course there are the large websites such as Rightmove and Zoopla.

Newspapers.

Daily Scottish newspapers are a good source of property. Regional and local newspapers carry many details on a regular basis.

Estate agents. These offer the same service

Home reports in Scotland

When you're buying a home in Scotland the seller will need to provide any potential buyers with a home report on their property. The only exceptions are new-builds and buildings that have recently been converted into residential properties. The home report consists of a single survey, an energy report and a property questionnaire.

The single survey contains a valuation and an assessment of the property's condition (including the roof, external walls and plumbing). You may want to consider getting a more detailed building survey done if the property is older or of a non-standard construction.

The energy report will give the property an energy efficiency rating and assess its environmental impact by looking at carbon dioxide emissions.

Completed by the seller, the property questionnaire will contain details such as whether the property has ever flooded or been treated for wood rot, as well as useful pieces of information such as what the parking arrangements are and which council tax band the home falls into.

Making an offer on a Scottish property

Properties in Scotland are usually marketed and sold by solicitors, rather than estate agents. They are either advertised at a fixed price or for 'offers around' or 'offers over' a certain price. When a property is advertised for 'offers around' or 'offers over', a closing date will be set and prospective purchasers will need to submit sealed bids before that date.

Your solicitor (see below) will work with you to prepare your offer and pass it on to the seller's solicitor on your behalf. As well as how much you're willing to pay for the property, your offer should include a proposed 'date of entry' – i.e. when you'll pay and get the keys - and other terms and conditions relating to the purchase.

Once the offers are in, the seller will then choose the offer they want to accept. No money is paid at this stage unless it's a new-build property, in which case a deposit may be required.

Conveyancing for buyers in Scotland

When buying a home in Scotland you'll need to instruct a solicitor very early on in the process. Once you've seen a property you're interested in buying, your solicitor should:

- Explain the home report to you
- Check that any alterations have been made with the necessary planning permission and building control approval
- Put together your offer with you
- Submit your offer to the seller's solicitor

Once the offers are in, the seller will choose the offer they want to accept. This doesn't have to be the highest.

If your bid is successful, your solicitor will confirm your mortgage with the lender, agree an entry date and deal with legal enquiries about the property.

Concluding the missives

They will also agree the contract with the seller's solicitor. This is known as 'concluding the missives', and it's legally binding for both the seller and buyer. At this point, the solicitor will undertake the conveyancing process to transfer the ownership of the property.

Settlement

On the date of entry that's agreed in the contract, you'll pay the whole of the purchase price in exchange for the keys to the property. This point is known as 'settlement'. Your solicitor will pay any LBTT (see below) that is due, register the change of ownership with the Registers of Scotland, and lodge title deeds with your mortgage lender (you'll get a copy too).

Land and Buildings Transaction Tax

Land and Buildings Transaction Tax (LBTT) is the Scottish equivalent of stamp duty and is charged on the following:

- First-time buyers: properties costing £175,000+
- Home movers: properties costing £145,000+
- Buy-to-let or second home buyers: properties costing £40,000+

For current LBTT rates go to:

https://www.gov.scot/policies/taxes/land-and-buildings-transaction-tax/

Buying a tenement property

Technically speaking, a tenement is a building or part of a building containing two or more flats that are separated horizontally and designed to have separate ownership. This includes houses converted into flats, high-rise blocks, and both traditional and modern buildings. Tenements can also be office blocks, although most are residential. More than a quarter of the housing in Scotland consists of tenements. If you're buying a flat in a tenement property, you will own your flat and a share of the tenement's common parts, and a share of the land upon which the tenement is built. The title deeds to each flat should set out who owns what. If the deeds don't do this, certain rules will apply - for example, the owner of the top-floor flat will own the roof space above it. Talk to your solicitor to find out how it works for the property you're buying. It's important that you fully understand the setup.

Tenement maintenance costs

As a tenement flat owner you're liable for a share of maintenance costs to common parts of the tenement. Unless the repairs are essential, a majority of the flat owners must agree on whether they are needed, which can cause difficulties and delays.

What is a 'factor'?

Sometimes the titles provide for the appointment of a 'factor'. This is a person or firm with the responsibility of managing and instructing repairs. If this isn't covered in the titles, the tenement owners may agree to appoint one. Assuming the factor acts properly, the owners of all the flats will be liable for the costs of repairs.

Restrictions of use

In Scotland, most property titles have conditions that restrict their use. For example, there will usually be a condition specifying that a property won't be used for commercial gains. When a property is passed to a new owner, so too are these conditions. Your solicitor will inform you of all title conditions involved with the property you're buying, normally prior to the date of entry but after the contract is concluded. If you're unhappy with any of the title conditions, you can try asking the seller to try getting the conditions changed. However, this rarely happens and the title conditions must usually be accepted for the deal to go ahead.

Feuhold properties and feu duty

This complex system was abolished for most properties in November 2004, but check with your solicitor to make sure it doesn't apply to your property.

Joint ownership of a Scottish property

If you want to buy a home with someone else, you have two options: joint ownership or common property. It's worth talking to your solicitor about what will work best for your situation before making a decision.

Joint ownership

If you've bought a house under joint ownership and one of you dies, your share will automatically pass to the other person without any conveyancing expense. Joint owners can sell or give away their share during their lifetime, but they can't give it away in a will.

Common property

If a home is owned as 'common property', the owners can sell or give away their share during their lifetime or in a will. This can be problematic if, for example, a couple has bought the property and then splits up. Your solicitor should explain all the consequences of these clauses before you decide to use one.

Help to Buy (Scotland)

This government scheme enables people to buy new-build homes with a deposit of 5%, government equity loan of 15% and mortgage of 80%. Help to Buy is currently set to run until March 2022 in Scotland. For more advice go to https://www.mygov.scot/help-to-buy.

How the Scottish property system differs from the rest of the UK

The property-buying process in Scotland is generally quicker and less likely to fall through than it can be in the rest of the UK, excluding Northern Ireland. In fact, research found that, in 2020, 10.4% of transactions fell through in Scotland after an offer had been accepted, compared to 21.8% in England, 22.9% in Wales, and 9.6% in Northern Ireland. There are a number of reasons for this:

- Preparing a home report costs money, therefore it's more likely that the vendor is serious about selling

- The home report means that buyers are better informed about a property's condition and value at the point of making an offer, so there's less potential for them to back out later

- Gazumping - when another buyer makes a higher offer after yours has been accepted - is rare because properties are usually withdrawn from the market once a price has been agreed. Solicitors are also not allowed to continue to represent a seller if they choose to go with a different buyer, meaning they don't encourage the practice.

It will generally take four to eight weeks to buy a property in Scotland, while it's more likely to take eight to 12 weeks in England, Northern Ireland or Wales.

****

Chapter 9

Buying Overseas

Thousands of Britons have purchased properties overseas. However, this can be problematic and certainly basic advice is needed relating to the particular country where you are buying. At this point in time, a lot of people with properties in EU countries are experiencing problems following BREXIT. Be very careful and be well informed when buying properties in EU countries (and anywhere else. Here are a few general tips when buying abroad:

- Buy through a qualified and licensed agent. In most countries including France, Spain, Portugal and the USA, agents legally have to be licensed and using an unlicensed agent means that there is no comeback if things go wrong.
- Do not sign anything until you are sure that you understand it. Note that estate agents in the above countries will tend to do more of the legal work than in Britain and hence charge more commission.
- Always hire a solicitor (English speaking if you are not fluent in the local language) to act for you. In some countries, the locals do not use solicitors but you should insist. The solicitor will check that the seller owns the property and that there are no

debts attached to it and that planning regulations have been met. Local searches are not as regulated as they are in the UK and it's often a case of making informal enquiries at the local town hall.

- Understand the role played by the state notary (notaire in France, notario in Spain) he or she is a state official, whose only role is to see that the sale is completed. He or she will not act for you or the seller.

There are a number of useful websites:

www.french-property-news.com

This site is the online arm of the magazine French Property News. It claims to have the most comprehensive list of properties on the web and also has details of other organisations.

www.french-property.com

For property in Spain, try www.homeespana.co.uk which specialises in all types of property including retirement property. For property in Eastern Europe you should go to www.eurobrix.com

For the USA-

www.primelocation.com

www.propertyshowrooms.com

www.escape2usa.co.uk

Property overseas generally

www.property-abroad.com

There are many other websites dealing with buying and selling property in most countries of the world. It goes without saying that you should learn as much about a country as possible and deal with professionals only before taking the plunge overseas.

****

Useful websites when buying and selling your home
The Buying Process-general

The Local Government Association

www.local.gov.uk

Confederation of Scottish Local Authorities

www.cosla.gov.uk

Greater London Authority

www.london.gov.uk

The Environment Agency

www.environment-agency.gov.uk

www.homecheckuk.com

House Prices

Halifax www.halifax.co.uk

Nationwide www.nationwide.co.uk

Land Registry www.landreg.gov.uk

www.zoopla.co.uk

www.ourproperty.co.uk

Property Search Sites

www.hometrack.co.uk

www.rightmove.co.uk

www.zoopla.co.uk

www.primelocation.com

www.onthemarket.com

www.home.co.uk

findahood.com

propertynetwork.net

findproperty.co.uk

propertyauctionaction.co.uk

uniquepropertybulletin.co.uk

The buying and selling process-law and taxation

The Law Society www.lawsoc.org.uk

The Council of Mortgage Lenders www.cml.org.uk

HM Revenue and Customs www.hmrc.gov

Scotland

Law Society of Scotland www.scotlaw.org.uk

Leasehold/freehold

Lease www.lease-advice.org

Association of Residential Managing Agents

www.arma.org.uk

Mortgage search sites/brokers

Money facts www.moneyfacts.co.uk

www.moneysupermarket.co.uk

www.moneynet.co.uk

New homes

NHBC www.nhbc.co.uk

Renting and Letting

Association of Residential Letting Agencies (ARLA)

Arbon House

6 Tournament Court

EdgeHill Drive

Warwick

CV34 6LG

Tel: 01926 496 800

Website: www.arla.co.uk

Email: help@propertymark.co.uk

Advice on taxation if you are considering letting out a property

www.which.co.uk/money/tax/income-tax/tax-on-property-and-rental-income/how-rental-income-is-taxed

www.gov.uk/guidance/income-tax-when-you-rent-out-a-property-working-out-your-rental-income

Auctions

www.primelocation.com

www.propertyauctions.com

propertyauctionaction.co.uk

****

Glossary of important terms when buying or selling a home

completion – when your legal representative transfers the remaining funds to the seller's legal representative and you take ownership of the property

conservation area – an area with extra planning controls to protect its special historic and architectural elements such as original windows or doors. These controls are tailored to each area by the council. Find out if these controls apply to your area by contacting your local planning authority.

conveyancer – legal executive, licensed conveyancer or conveyancing solicitor who does the legal work to do with transferring the ownership of land or buildings from one person to another. They will generally owe a duty to their client to take reasonable care when carrying out that legal work.

credit score – a rating showing how likely a lender is to lend you money.

decision in principle – a written statement from a lender to say that 'in principle' they would lend a certain amount to a particular prospective borrower.

deposit – a payment passed on to your legal representative upon exchange of contracts, which represents a percentage of the purchase price.

Energy Performance Certificate (EPC) – an Energy Label with a ranking of between A and G that also indicates running costs and suggests suitable improvements which can be made to a property to make it more energy efficient. An EPC must be provided to any potential buyer unless the property is exempt from EPC requirements.

exchange of contracts – when contracts are exchanged between buyers and sellers. Legally binding and commits the parties to the property sale/purchase.

estate facility charge (service or maintenance charges) – an annual fee for maintaining the wider estate on which a property is located, e.g. for upkeep of public areas.

fittings – items in your property that are not fixed down e.g. carpets, curtain rails, free-standing ovens, fridges, freezers and washing machines.

fixtures – items in your property that are fixed to the floor or wall, e.g. light fittings, built-in wardrobes, boiler, radiators, plug sockets.

freehold – where you own the land and the buildings on it outright.

ground rent – a payment generally made annually by the leaseholder to the freeholder under the terms of a lease. Historically many ground rents are set at a minimal 'peppercorn' rate; but it is also common for the lease to provide that the ground rent increases at intervals. For example, initial ground rent of £100 per annum going up after 33 years to £150 p.a. and after 66 years increasing finally to £200 p.a. However, there can be substantially higher increases and more regular changes, so the amount and any consequential changes should be understood at an early stage.

home survey – a report to advise clients on the condition and matters relating to a property.

HM Land Registry the organisation which registers the ownership of land and property in England and Wales.

indemnity insurance – insurance that can be used during conveyancing transactions to cover a legal defect with the property that can't be quickly resolved, or at all.

lease – a document which sets out the rights and duties of landlord, leaseholder and any other party, such as a management company, who has rights and obligations in the lease.

leasehold – where you own the right to occupy a property for a fixed number of years, typically 99 years or more.

letter of engagement – sets out the terms of agreement between the client and their legal representative including client instruction, fees, timescales and other relevant information.

listed building – listing marks a building's special architectural and historic interest and brings it under the protection of the planning system. Depending on the category of listed building and the scope of alterations a householder may wish to make, listed building consent will need to be secured to make any changes that might affect the building's special interest. More details are available on the Historic England website.

local authority searches – a set of information about a property and/or land and the local area provided by the relevant authority.

LPE1 form – contains information about a property held by landlords, managing agents and management companies – for example, information on ground rent and service charges.

mortgage valuation – an assessment made by your mortgage provider as to whether they are willing to lend you money against a property. This is not the same thing as a survey.

ombudsman – an official organisation appointed to investigate individual's complaints against a company or organisation.

property chain – linked property transactions, where a seller of one property is a buyer of another.

property searches – a legal professional will conduct legal searches when you are buying a property to ensure there are no other factors you should be aware of. Some searches will be recommended by your legal representative for all purchases and others will be required by the mortgage lender to protect them from any liabilities that the property may have.

redress scheme – all estate agents are legally required to be members of a redress scheme. Schemes may be able to resolve disputes between estate agents and consumers once internal complaint processes have been exhausted. More information is available from the government's website.

referral fee – a payment made from one business to another in exchange for referring customers to them.

reservation fee – a payment made to a developer to secure a property.

service charge – A contribution payable by a leaseholder typically to a freeholder or managing agent, for a share of the cost of insuring, maintaining, repairing, and cleaning the building.

snagging – defects or unfinished pieces of work in a new build home.

sold subject to contract (SSTC) – an offer has been made on the property and the seller has accepted it, but they have yet to exchange, so it is not legally binding.

stamp duty/Land Transaction Tax – a tax paid upon purchase of any homes costing more than £125,000 in England (or £180,000 in Wales), unless you are a first time buyer.

(home) survey – an agreed level of service to advise clients on the condition and matters relating to a property. The homebuyer's survey should not be confused with a mortgage valuation.
purchasing a property.

title – a legal document signifying ownership of a property.

under offer – the same as 'sold subject to contract' – an offer has been made on the property and the seller has accepted it, but they have yet to exchange contracts, so it is not legally binding.

Index

Architects and Surveyors Institute, 35
Area, 3, 13, 116
Areas of Outstanding Natural Beauty, 23
Association of Building
Auctions, 5, 60

Bankruptcy, 9, 126
Bidding for a, 5, 65rs, 35
Brokers, 6, 72
Budgeting, 4, 48
Building Guarantees, 3, 25
Building societies, 71
Buildings insurance, 5, 56
Buildings of architectural or historical interest, 22
Buy to Let Mortgages, 7, 85
Buying a listed building, 3, 22
Buying abroad, 141
Buying an old house, 3, 20
Buying at auction, 61
Buying Overseas, 141
Buying with a friend, 5, 60

Cashbacks, 7, 85
Centralised lenders, 6, 72
Chartered Institute of Arbitrators 020 7421 7455, 90
Choosing your property, 3, 14
Coal mining search, 8, 116

Commonhold, 16, 17, 106

Commonhold and Leasehold Reform Act 2002, 16, 17

Commons Registration Act (1965) search, 116

Completing a sale, 5, 60

Completion, 9, 124

Conservation areas, 23

Contract for sale, 8, 118

Conveyancing, 8, 52, 103

Costs of moving, 5, 57

Covenants, 106

COVID 19, 11

Death of Vendor, 9, 126

Deposit, 4, 48

Deposits, 6, 77

Developers, 62

Disabled facilities grant, 3, 21

Endowment, 7, 82

Energy Performance Certificates, 5, 53

Energy Performance Certificates (EPC's), 5, 53

English Heritage, 22

Equalities Act 2010, 3, 21

Estate Agents, 4, 15, 33, 35, 48

Exchange of contracts, 5, 59

Exchanging contracts, 8, 123

Finance, 6, 68

Financial advisers, 71

Financial advisors, 6, 72
Financial Ombudsman Service, 90
Financial Services Act 1986, 118
Flipping, 62
Forced sales, 63
Foreign currency mortgages, 7, 84
Freehold property, 8, 104
French Property News, 142

Georgian Group, 20
Ground rents, 63

Halifax, 15, 42
Heat Pumps, 11
Help to Buy equity loan, 6
Help to Buy Scheme, 4, 6, 29
Historic Scotland, 22
House swapping, 6, 69

Incorporated Society of Valuers and Auctioneers, 35
Interest only mortgage, 7, 84
investment properties, 63

Joint mortgages, 6, 82
Joint sole agents, 4, 36

Land Certificate, 8, 110, 111
Land Registration Acts of 1925, 109
Land Registry, 5, 15, 52, 57, 109, 110, 111, 144

Law of Property Act (Miscellaneous provisions) 1988, 118
Leasehold, 145
Leasehold property, 8, 105
Leasehold Reform Act 1993, 17
Legal ownership of property, 8, 103
Legal pack, 67
Lenders, 6, 68, 71, 73, 77, 89
Local authority properties, 63
Local authority searches, 8, 115
Local Land Charges Act 1975, 113
Local land charges search, 8, 111, 113

Making an offer, 5, 58
Misdescription, 8, 120
Misrepresentation, 8, 121, 122
Mixed mortgages, 7, 84
Mortgage, 68
Mortgage arrangement fees, 5, 55
Mortgage fees, 5, 55
Mortgage indemnity insurance, 5, 55
Mortgage Market Review, 6
Multiple agency, 4, 36

National Energy Services Scheme, 24
Non-disclosure, 8, 122

Pension mortgages, 7, 84
Planning permission, 3, 21
Probates, 63

Property investors, 62
Property Misdescriptions Act 2010, 34
Purchasing a flat, 3, 15

Receivership sales, 63
Registered land, 8, 109
Removals, 5, 56
Removers, 130
Renovation grants, 3, 20
Repayment mortgages, 7, 83
Repossessions, 62, 63
Right to Buy, 3, 26, 27
Royal Institute of British Architects, 20
Royal Institute of Chartered, 15, 20
Royal Institute of Chartered Surveyors, 15, 20
Rural areas, 13

Scotland, 9, 22, 80, 133, 145
Secretary of State for National Heritage, 22
Secretary of State for Scotland, 22
Secretary of State for Wales, 22
Self-build, 4, 30
Service charges, 16
Services, 24, 89, 90, 118
Shared ownership property, 4, 29
Social Homebuy, 3, 28
Social Housing, 29
Sole agency selling., 4, 35
Spain, 141, 142

Special Conditions of Sale, 67
Stamp duty, 4, 49, 57
Stamp Duty, 49, 89
Structural surveys, 5, 53

The 1996 Housing Act, 16
The National House Building Council, 24
Transport links, 13

Urban areas, 13
USA, 10, 141, 142

Valuing a property, 3, 15
Victorian Society, 20
Viewing properties, 3, 19

Yuppification, 13

****